Love Intelligence

*LoveQ– Coaching for modern women
(the 2-nd edition, improved and enlarged)*

OKSANA SHMID

GreatWriters
MEDIA

Inquiries and Book Orders should be addressed to:

Great Writers Media
Email: info@greatwritersmedia.com
Phone: 877-600-5469

ISBN: 978-1-960605-83-2 (sc)
ISBN: 978-1-960605-84-9 (ebk)

Library of Congress Control Number: 2022917748

Contents

I express my most heartfelt thanks to...

... My beloved man for taking on the role of my muse. Thanks for the invaluable experience!

... My parents who have always believed in me and supported me in everything.

... My clients whose success and gratitude please me and stimulate me to constantly develop.

I express special gratitude to my colleagues (Anton Semenov, Angela Yastreb, Svetlana Zhovnirenko, Itskhak Pintosevich, Alunika Dobrovolskaya, Lydia Shpakovskaya-Radichi), whose wisdom and support helped me to write this book and to progress as a coach and psychologist!

I am grateful to God for both the trials and the fortunes that contributed to my success.

Thanks to my friends and everyone who helped me to create this book.

You all fill my life with love. And that means you give me a sense of purpose!

Sincerely yours,
Oksana Schmid

My dear reader!

Apparently, you are planning to change your life drastically, because LoveQ coaching is convenient not for everyone, but only for determined and purposeful ones.

I want to congratulate you - it is in this book that you will find everything you need to align your knowledge of Love.

During my practice as a coach and a psychologist, I encountered so many identical mistakes that I decided to tell how girls can finally stop doing stupid things and, using clear and effective coaching tools, get rid of the chaos in their thoughts and put the desired order in their personal lives.

I have identified three of the most important problems that prevent girls from loving and being loved. And if you do not have the desired happiness in your personal life yet then the reason, anyway, lies in them.

- Lack of self-knowledge and lack of an inspiring goal. We have desires, we have even dreams - but we don't have any worthwhile realistic goal. We chase socially approved ideals and sometimes lose ourselves behind the masks of invented roles.

- Lack of knowledge of relationships and love psychology. Conflicting, superficial information is even worse than its lack. Before becoming an expert in something, you need to study information about the subject, that is, objects of personal life. A clear, harmonious system of knowledge is the basis of LoveQ coaching.

- Lack of systematic actions. In no other area of life, there are so many questions about the worthwhileness of activity as in the area of personal life. It seems to all of us that "they will come and give everything themselves." And we forget that these words were said by Woland (I remind, that he embodied the image of the devil in Bulgakov's novel) to Margarita, and he a priori cannot be interested in women's happiness.

But everything is fixable. Do not worry, in nature everything is harmonious, everything is balanced, everything is 50 to 50. And every girl will definitely find her significant other. Don't give up hope, even after several failed attempts.

This book will definitely help you to change your personal life for the better. And if you know what you want, believe in success, and act, then success is inevitable.

I believe that miracles are possible in real life, but they are preceded by a lot of effort, determination, and belief in your dreams!

My life can serve you as an example of dreams coming true. However, only if you do not sit idle and clearly know what you need, and don't settle for less.

There was a time when I, like you, dreamed of luxury resorts, reputation, a millionaire husband, and my own business. I was born in an ordinary family of modest means, and without my innate (or acquired) will to win my dreams would, probably, have remained dreams.

For the first time, I got married very early, at the age of 18, to a guy a little older than me, I moved to him in another city. And, as often happens, after a while, it became obvious that we had different outlooks on life. After 8 years of marriage, we broke up when we realized that a compromise was no longer possible.

So, I came back to Kyiv, where my parents lived. And after a luxurious life and success (I just launched my career as a TV presenter on regional Kharkiv television, was actively developing the advertising business), I found myself without a livelihood in a small rented apartment on the outskirts of Kyiv.

I had to work hard and study. It was difficult - my ambitions clearly exceeded my capabilities.

Sometimes I gave up, I wanted the Prince, but only "frogs" came way, and those who I liked, for some reason were not interested in me.

I have forgotten to say that my weight was about 70 kg and, as you understand, I did not have money for luxurious clothes. I also belonged to the category of girls who loved very much. As soon as I liked a young man, I immediately tried my best to catch his fancy, and in the end, he did not fall in love. And thus, after another romantic disappointment, in a flood of tears, I promised myself never to fall in unrequited love again! I decided to be happy! I sat down and wrote all my dreams and started acting. I entered the university at the Faculty of Psychology, attended one training after another, listened to affirmations every day, signed up with a fitness club, and found a new job.

The kilograms quickly dwindled, and self-confidence grew. I changed my style, and instead of a pile of old clothes, I had two decent Italian suits and three dresses in my wardrobe. I inquired about the city's marriage agencies and started dating. And one day I met my prince - a handsome millionaire from Germany. He proposed marriage to me at our fifth meeting. And if I omit the description of the efforts that I put into this, then we can say that I was just lucky!

I am very grateful to my second husband. Next to him, I succeeded as a business lady, traveled half of the world, learned several foreign languages - it was an amazing period in my life. My husband even built a castle for us. I still don't understand where our mutual love has gone ... But it happens sometimes.

The divorce was followed by several failed financial deals, and I had to start everything practically all over again.

Yes, my life can hardly be called boring or easy, it is more like a Brazilian TV series with a plot that is traditional for such films. There were many different things in it: both good and bad. But even in the most difficult moments, I kept repeating to myself: "God never sends trials that you are not able to overcome!" And I went forward, trying not to look for those responsible for my troubles, not digging into the past, but gaining experience for growth and development.

Close friends often, lovingly, call me "The Phoenix Bird". I manage to rebirth with renewed vigor after vicissitudes of life and live in a state of tranquility and positiveness. I learned to set goals and achieve them, to believe in a dream, to smile at life, to overcome obstacles and my own doubts!

Fundamentally, Success and Luck are different things. Success is the number of times when a person manages to overcome circumstances, doubts, and most importantly, himself and, continuing to believe in destiny, to pursue his cherished goal.

I am in no way claiming to be a love guru because I married a millionaire or because I know how to charm men. But my professional and life experience and, most importantly, the successes of my clients and students permit me to assert that LoveQ coaching techniques work great and really allow you to get rid of the chaos in your head and personal life, to find deserved happiness.

Keep believing in destiny and pursuing your cherished goal.

The road to success is challenging but worth it. You need just a little perseverance and practice, and everything will be as you dream. And my knowledge will just help you along the way!

About LoveQ Coaching

The theme of love has always been very interesting to me. I tried to find secrets allowing to arouse a feeling of amorousness, first for myself, and then I began to share my findings with clients. In such a way the whole comprehensive program of love intelligence LoveQ development appeared.

Creating it, I thought about how to help you in this difficult task - the search for the Man of Dreams, how to guard you against illusions and idle hopes, disappointments, and instead of this to give clear guidelines in life, self-confidence and belief that everything is possible, you should just really want it.

During my professional practice as a psychologist and coach, I noted two main problems because of which people turn to experts: failures in financial and personal life. It is the dissatisfaction in these areas that robs our life of brightness, joy, and a feeling of self-fulfillment. And often it is the problems in the love department that interfere with career achievements.

It is not surprising. It is difficult to imagine a truly happy life without Love. It is the love that gives us a sense of purpose and the most pleasant emotions.

According to the research by Diener and Seligman, all those who joined the 10% of the happiest representatives of humanity were romantically involved at the time of the survey.

The ability to love and to be loved is an integral part of human happiness and life harmony.

However, not all of us have this great ability. This is a talent!

As well as with any other talent, people are divided into those who inherited it from birth, and those who need to make an effort to develop this feeling. In order to develop a love intelligence, it is necessary to master special knowledge and skills.

To make my consultations more effective and useful, I began to study the sphere of relationships deeper and deeper. Perseverance, wise books, seminars, trainings, deep professional knowledge of psychology, my personal life experience, and the great results of my clients created me as a specialist and expert in relationships.

For me, the result is very important in life and work, therefore, when I first encountered real coaching, I realized that I had found the perfect method for my purposeful nature, and began to gradually apply it in my practice.

I understood that it was an ideal tool for solving business problems, but I began to think about how to use it for success in personal life.

Once I found in a popular psychology book (the market of which I carefully study) by Dr. Kurpatov a Formula for Success in Life, and it was the following: ***"Take work as flirting, and flirting as work"***. He explained that to take flirting (personal life, love, the formation of sincere relations) as work means to understand the importance, seriousness of these relations for you; to remember that another person is another person, and that's why you should build relations carefully, respecting and recognizing his individuality; to be aware that there will be no quick results, that any work involves a serious investment of forces and resources; and finally, it is necessary to love this work, otherwise nothing will get done. It fully confirmed my belief that it is coaching that can help people who dream of individual happiness. Indeed, why not to apply a reasonable approach to searching for your soul mate, to treat the issue wisely?

LoveQ coaching has become my forte in work with clients. I am sure that dedicated specialists are necessary for solving particular problems. For example, you would prefer to have an operation performed by a surgeon rather than by a therapeutist, even if he has an excellent reputation. And in coaching for solving problems in your personal life, it is better to choose a relationship specialist with a good knowledge of the laws of the human mind as your coach.

There was little information about LOVE coaching and it was mostly in English. I bought my first book on LOVE coaching in America. I began to create my own tools to achieve goals in my personal life, I saw the first successes of my clients and firmly decided to devote my activities to the research and development of this direction.

This is how the idea of creating a whole direction in coaching, a system for the development of love intelligence, a comprehensive program for the qualitative improvement of Personal Life LoveQ-SCHOOL, the synergy of coaching, psychotherapy, and modern neuropsychology appeared.

How love intelligence contributes to individual happiness?

Love intelligence is the ability to handle effectively the love sphere of human life, to understand the other and yourself in relationships, and use your knowledge to solve problems in your personal life.

Usual behavioral trainings, which teach the right way to behave, offer tactical rather than strategic decisions, do not give a keen understanding of yourself, your own motives and experience, clear omnifarious knowledge. The excitement after such trainings lasts for a week, and the worldview can be completely reprogrammed by someone else's techniques that do not work for you. For example, a dress that is a good fit for your friend may not suit you at all. My LoveQ-coaching system is about good taste, how to create your own unique image of success and happiness, and how to figure out what "suits personally you".

I help bridge gaps in education and develop critical thinking in romantic life - as the ability to choose independently the most appropriate strategies of thinking and behavior for you.

The program has helped many women find their unique road to individual happiness and protect themselves from fatal mistakes, because of which they often do not find or lose love. I am sure that LoveQ coaching will help you too.

Love! Make fall in love! You are worthy of Love and Happiness!

LoveQ-TEST: define your "love intelligence"

This is a simple test the passing of which takes only 5-7 minutes.
You will find out your position on 12 basic competencies that affect the building of a happy personal life.

After passing the test, you will know exactly to which competence you should pay maximum attention.

1. Clearness of goal

a) I do not achieve my goals.

b) I do not see any reason to set specific goals in my life, I hardly ever achieve what I want.

c) I dream of happiness in my personal life, but I don't fully understand what kind of partner I need.

d) I perfectly understand what I want, but I do not have written goals and a plan to achieve them.

e) I perfectly understand what I want, the goals are noted down and I have a clear plan to achieve them.

2. Ability to manage your emotions

a) It is easy to offend me, I often feel sorry for myself.

b) Usually, I tolerate everything and sort things out only when I'm boiling over.

c) I try to understand what the other person feels in the relationship, and not to offend him with my demands or embarrass him with emotions.

d) I try to control my emotions and wait for the right moment to express my thoughts.

e) I do not store up resentment, I immediately say if I like or dislike something, estimating only the behavior of the person that induced my reaction.

3. Behavioral agility

a) Similar stories always repeat in relationships with me, I step on the same "romantic rake".

b) I always find partners with the same disadvantages, hoping that they will change.

c) It's probably my own fault that I can not learn from past mistakes.

d) I understand that I am attracted to unsuitable partners, I realize it and draw conclusions for the future.

e) I easily change my behavior according to the situation and always get what I want.

4. Energy, inspiration, and enthusiasm

a) I don't know what I want and that's why I don't feel inspired.

b) Sometimes I have a desire to change something, but everyday routine often absorbs all the enthusiasm.

c) I have a constant desire to change something in my personal life, but I do not understand what exactly I should do.

d) I am full of determination to achieve my goals.

e) I quietly and confidently go towards my goals, everything is developing in the best way for me.

5. Perseverance, activity

a) I do nothing to achieve goals in my personal life.

b) It is a partner who should be active, he will find me.

c) I try not to miss the opportunities that I see.

d) I regularly try to improve my personal life, but somehow chaotically.

e) I am actively involved in organizing my personal life, go on first dates, and know that sooner or later I will meet the right partner for me.

6. Potential

a) Now I have no time for personal life.

b) I still do not have enough time, funds, acquaintanceship, knowledge, I am not self-confident enough to meet the partner of my dreams.

c) I do not have everything I need to succeed in love yet, but I'm looking for opportunities.

d) I have access to all basic resources: money, time, information, skills, acquaintanceship, for individual happiness building.

e) I have everything in abundance and I am ready for a meeting and relationship with the Man of my dreams.

7. Cheerfulness and optimism

a) I am often sad, now I am depressed.

b) Everything seems to be good, but there is no feeling of life.

c) I worry about something all the time, but I hope for the best.

d) Mostly I'm in a good mood.

e) I am an optimist, I am easy to get on with and fun to be with.

8. External attractiveness

a) I do not like myself and nobody likes me.

b) I have a normal appearance.

c) I am attractive enough, but not 100% satisfied with myself.

d) In appearance, I correspond to my ideas about the ideal woman in almost everything.

e) I am the best!

9. Confidence in your feminine attractiveness, ability to make fall in love

a) Nobody has ever fallen in love with me.

b) I am not pampered with attention.

c) I usually fall in love first.

d) People like me, sometimes they fall in love with me.

e) People always fall in love with me.

10. Creativity, imagination, naughtiness

a) I do not know what to do at my leisure, I am usually bored.

b) I wait for someone to think of something to do.

c) I like watching TV in my free time or surfing the Internet, I have no special hobbies.

d) I am an enthusiastic person, I have many different interests.

e) I easily find original leisure ideas for myself and my friends, it is always interesting to be with me.

11. Influence, ability to get what you want

a) I never get what I want in a relationship.

b) I can rarely assert my rights in a relationship.

c) I try to convince my partner, to prove my case in order to get what is beneficial for me.

d) I manage to negotiate with a partner.

e) I always get what I want in a relationship.

12. Understanding the opposite sex psychology

a) I don't understand men at all.

b) It seems to me that it is difficult for us to find a common language.

c) Members of the opposite sex perceive me as a friend, but not as a woman.

d) People are all different, regardless of gender.

e) I understand gender differences well in behavior.

Most answers A and B - you have low love intelligence.

You are a vulnerable and touchy person. You often choose partners who hurt you or, perhaps, try to avoid new love disappointments. But you need to be loved and admired, and you deserve a better fate.

You are often unjust to yourself. And although you have weaknesses, you can neutralize them. If you want to live a happy and harmonious life, now you need new knowledge and skills, and in the ideal case, you need the support of more experienced real friends who believe in you.

Don't be lazy and don't look to blame for your failures! Understand yourself, your main internal and external obstacles, and take responsibility for your destiny into your own hands. Treat yourself with love, and you will see how others will begin to feel more and more sympathy with you.

Most answers D and E - you have high love intelligence

Congratulations! In many ways, you are really strong, and if there are growth zones, it is just a matter of time for you. You know how to make a good choice in any life situation, you set goals and achieve them.

You do not like restrictions and pales, you prefer to make deliberate decisions on your own. And if your personal life is not 10 out of 10, then you can easily balance it.

You are a wise and mature person - you will succeed in everything!

Most answers are B and C, all other options - you have average love intelligence.

You often think that you deserve better. You seem to be a very purposeful person, but inside you are full of doubts: whether you have chosen the right road, whether you are good enough ... Sometimes you are too trusting, but you try to learn from your mistakes. There is a possibility of underestimating your capabilities, so already today understand your strong suit, and rely on them as on the basis of your confidence.

It's time to move from dreams to setting goals, it's time to understand what you really need in your personal life. After all, you have almost everything you need to be happy in love. A little rethinking will help you become more aware of your real goals and become more effective.

Organization and consistency will give results, and you will surprise yourself. You are worthy of beautiful love and happiness, do not settle for less.

12 Basic LoveQ Coaching Lessons

1. **Choose your future.** What comes true in life is what your thoughts and attention are focused on.

2. **Play by your own rules.** Manage the situation, otherwise, the situation will begin to manage you.

3. **Decide who you want to become.** And become!

4. **Fall in love with yourself!** Treat yourself the way you would like your boyfriend to treat you.

5. **Be cheerful!** Of all women, men choose the most cheerful. Of the cheerful - the most beautiful. Of the beautiful - the wisest.

6. **Change yourself!** If you want to change the situation, change your behavior in it. If you want to change a person, change yourself.

7. **Better be born ambitious than rich.** Take action!

8. **Take failures lightly.** Learn from them and just move on. Quantity always turns into quality.

9. **A relationship is not a goal in itself, but a process.** Enjoy the process!

10. **You are the best!** Not one of the best. Always remember about it.

11. **Fall in love wisely!** Love to the hilt!

12. **Be wiser!** Achieve success with two the most important words: love and kindness!

LESSON 1

Choose your future!

What comes true in life is what your thoughts and attention are focused on You purchased this book in order to become happier in your personal life. Let's clarify what "Happiness" is, and thus take the first decisive step towards it. According to the results of numerous studies, we can safely say that everyone has his own happiness, and its coefficient and definition directly depend on what this particular person needs, what he wants and what he dreams of. The following definition is very close to me: happiness is when my capability, desire, and duties are equal.

The happiness formula in coaching is the following:

To intend to be happy + to move towards this =
= to experience true happiness.

We live in a sense of harmony with ourselves when we are in the process of fulfilling desires. If we have everything going for us and we succeed in many things, we are calm and proud of ourselves and live in anticipation of something good.

To be - to do - to have!

To begin with, focus your attention on who you are and on your dearest wishes, then start moving towards their fulfillment, learning to manage your thoughts, feelings, and actions, that is, your attention, and very soon you will receive fate's gift in the form of Happiness in personal life.

To grow fond of your dreams and to learn how to achieve your goals is what you should start your road to happiness from. You need, finally, to realize what you want and what you can do for this, to learn to control your destiny, and therefore to control yourself in the first place. And you will see how your life gradually will become as you want, more freedom of choice and opportunities will appear.

INFORMATION FOR REFLECTION
According to most researchers, one of the most successful interpretations of the concept of personal (private) life belongs to Yu.A. Zamoshkin:

*- **firstly**, it is the inner spiritual life. Recognition of a person's sovereignty in the world of his thoughts and feelings, freedom to think in one way or another, to believe in one thing, but not to believe in another, to experience some feelings;*
*- **secondly**, this is the sphere of interpersonal communication, the right of a person to build relationships himself, to decide who is worthy of his respect and who is worthy of his contempt, who to love or not love, with whom to enter into sexual or friendly relations, and who to avoid.*

Where does happiness live?

So, we know that a person is happy when he moves towards his goal. And the goal of LoveQ coaching is happiness in your personal life. The path to it is not always easy, but it is always exciting, and those who overcome it will receive the major prize - the love of the man of their dreams.

Success Rule No 1. Know Your Goal!
First, you need to know yourself and your real needs and stimulating dreams and understand what kind of man is capable of making you really happy. As the ancients said, for a ship that does not know where to sail, no wind will be favorable.

Success Rule No 2. Get Faith!
Each of us lives in two worlds: inner and external. In the inner world, there are our thoughts, feelings, experiences, in the external -

events and our reactions. As a rule, we react to an external stimulus with inner experiences and thoughts. Realize your worldview and self-determination, what you believe in now, because "according to your faith will it be done to you". It is your thoughts and belief in the success that form your reactions and, as a result, your own reality.

What if the world can begin to change, adapting to you, to your thoughts? This is how successful people live. First, an idea appears inside them, there it acquires a visual picture, they begin to think and dream about it, to act, regardless of difficulties. And then everything conceived comes into fruition. Believe in yourself and your dreams. Start living as if miracles are possible and they will definitely happen. The thought is primary. Create your desired future with your thoughts! Discipline your thinking, inculcate new mental habits in you - and you will be happy!

SMILE

A man dies and gets to Paradise. Angels meet him in Heaven and say: "Listen, man, of course, you will go to Paradise, but first we will show you how you could live on earth." They approach a three-storey villa with palm trees around it, on the Mediterranean sea coast: "All this could be yours." Man: "Ooh-ooh." They move on. There is a fleet of cars, among them there is Mercedes, Bentley, Ferrari, and many others: "All this could be yours." Man: "Ooh-ooh." They go ahead: a woman sits, beautiful, intelligent, the best woman on earth: "And she could be yours." Man: "Oooh ... Why wasn't it?" "Because you kept harping on the same thing: I want Zaporozhets, I want Zaporozhets!"

Success Rule No 3. Take Action!

That makes sense. Understand what kind of woman will correspond to the conception of the ideal chosen one for the Man of your dreams, and from that moment start to improve yourself. And not for him, but for yourself.

Become the fairy of your life!

It makes no sense to constantly look back at the past, regret missed opportunities, sorting through the heaps of memories. There is "today and now" to focus your energy on what you really want. Focus on your dream! Seven coaching skills will help you. It is useful to foster them for the easier fruition of your dreams. Learn to ask yourself the right questions at the appropriate times, and you will be able to control your attention, thoughts, fate, start "living as you dream, and not as luck would have it".

SMILE
- I don't go to the gym on Mondays.
- But why?
- You see, many people start a new life on Mondays, so I come on Tuesday - their new life has already ended, and the gym is empty.

Become a fairy of your life and be able to transform:

1. Problems into tasks

Live with passion and be able to transform any life problems into tasks. Instead of meaningless complaints, ask yourself the question: "HOW do I want and HOW can I solve this task? What opportunities do I have before me?"

2. Tasks into game

Transform a difficult task into an exciting game with many possibilities. Try different moves. Ask yourself: "What are the options for solving the task?" Play "as if". For example, if you want to become someone or have something, then you should start acting as if this has already happened.

Even if you do not have all the necessary resources to implement your plans yet, start acting on the basis of the available ones.

Remember, the best day to start is today!

3. Doubts into decisions

You need to think and discuss when making decisions, and having decided on the task, start acting. That is, don't think anymore WHAT to do, but think HOW to do.

A Japanese proverb says: "After thinking, decide, but after deciding, don't think!" Excessive immersion in thoughts creates doubts and taxes vitality. What matters in life is what we feel and do. Respect your decisions!

4. Pessimism into optimism

Optimists have their dreams come true, pessimists have their nightmares come true. Thoughts with a plus sign! Learn to see the joy in small things, to notice good points in yourself, in others, in the world. Thanks to cognitive distortions, it is easier for our brain to notice bad things, it does it in autopilot mode, but the joy must be noticed consciously. And this is a special wisdom that happy people have.

Always look for good and beautiful things around you, and you do not need to wait for special events, circumstances to enjoy life. Ask yourself more often questions during the day: "What good do I notice in this situation, person, myself? What do I express gratitude for? What does please me here and now? "

Replace "No way out! I can not!" with "What if there was a better way out? What options are possible? What resources do I already have and what can I get? "

5. Fear into inspiration

The embodiment of your wildest desires is usually at the door marked "Fear". A person cannot be afraid and act at the same time. Take action, the anxiety will go away, and you will feel a surge of energy and inspiration.

MINUTE OF WISDOM
Chance favors the prepared mind.
Louis Pasteur

6. "It is necessary" into "I want"

Real, often unconscious desires always win, and if not, then the person feels unhappy. Therefore, first, do what you want, and do not do what you do not want. Live in the manner of "I Want!" and not "I must!".

You need to work on your self-esteem, understand and know yourself, feel your true desires, and look for opportunities to implement them, and not to dismiss them.

7. Failures into wisdom

Take failures and unluck as an important life experience! The universe never sends us trials for no reason. Instead of "WHY is it happening to me?", ask yourself the question: "WHY am I given this situation? What important thing can this teach me?"

How to achieve your goals easily?

If you are determined to have a lasting positive result in your personal life, then tactical recommendations "what to do" and "what to say" will not help. You need smart strategies and well-developed personal skills that all women who fall in love and fall in love easily, have. With such women it is always interesting, they are able to surprise, intrigue, give hope. They are attractive, seductive, and at the same time sincere, because they are real, and they usually say what they think and do what they like, and as a result, they get what they want. How to become such a woman?

Get inspired by your dream!

Learn to dream with passion. Self-confident people who know what they want attract us like a magnet. They live with passion, and this passion is passed on to us. We follow those who are more inspired than we are. We follow those whose dream is bigger.

Don't limit your dream to reality. A dream lives outside of logic, it, like faith, is a guest from the emotional sphere of our unconscious, and it is our unconscious that actually guides our desires.

Love your dreams unconditionally, they inspire and fill your life with meaning! The task of a dream is to show the potential of your personality, you in future, your opportunities, life direction, and launch the laws of attraction in your destiny. A dream is always large-scale and we need it to create the power of intention, to visualize our potential, and to explore the "Ideal Me".

Do not analyze "if it is possible or impossible, if it will be successful or not", just create an attractive picture of the future for your unconscious, which will help you keep the focus of attention on the desired future, will form the right direction in the invisible quantum world of the multivariance of your destiny. Developing your imagination, you will enter into resonance with the quantum world of the universe. I know it sounds mystical. But all great accomplishments began with a belief in a dream, often an unreasonable dream from the point of view of logic. For example, Sara Blakely, the founder of Spanx company, who became the youngest female billionaire, is a big fan of visualization. She imagined herself on The Oprah Winfrey Show 15 years before she appeared there.

Visualization develops a creative approach to life. Robert Stone's theory is that fantasizing in a relaxed state activates the right hemisphere of the brain - the source of creativity and ingenious decisions.

Dream emotionally. Fill the dream with the emotions of admiration, pleasure, inspiration and gratitude, explore it, detail it, notice new nuances. Our brain believes only in what it can imagine, see, it trusts and strives for what it likes and what evokes positive emotions.

Visualize actions! Not only the result, not only the things that you would like to have, but competencies, skills, situations. The human brain's ability to learn is so great that even if you just imagine the desired actions, it "turns on" activity in the areas responsible for training the skills that you need to have in order to achieve what you want. Your unconscious is not able to distinguish between real and imagined experiences, so it will be easier for you to perform planned actions later.

Visualize how you easily and with pleasure overcome obstacles on your way, that is, how you show your best features, become stronger. Before going to bed, imagine in detail your ideal tomorrow and how you go through obstacles. Believe me, it will come true.

Every day visualize your "Ideal Me". What you often think about and what you imagine begins to change. And first of all, you change yourself, you become the best version of yourself. Describing and imagining your story of happiness, you seem to be creating a video of the happy end of your success, you help your unconscious to choose automatically the right life strategies, and you will become more confident and decisive optimist day after day.

Get a dream talisman. It may be in the form of a bracelet, pendant, or keychain to remind you again and again of your dream and regular visualization.

INFORMATION FOR REFLECTION

In a survey conducted by psychologists Robert Emmons and Michael McCullough, it was found that people who kept a gratitude diary and every day wrote in it at least five things for which they were grateful to fate, could boast of higher levels of spiritual welfare and physical health. Start your own "Diary of Joy". During the day note small and big joys. Every night before going to bed, write down at least five things that have made or are making you happy.

MINUTE OF WISDOM
A young hasid said to rabbi Leib:
- I looked at this world: what a horror!
Rabbi Leib said:
- And who told you that you saw the world? You saw your reflection in it.
Jewish parable

Checklist: the golden rules for effective visualization

- Visualize when you want to revive yourself of energy and positivity.

- Focus your attention on the dream and enjoy what you see. Fill your visualization with emotions of joy, admiration, and inspiration.

-Visualize in complete peace, so that no one interferes. Preliminarily bring your breathing into harmony: inhale, hold your breath, exhale deeply, complete relaxation (5-6 times).

- During visualization, the head should be thrown back, the gaze - directed upward to the right, 15–20 degrees above the horizon line, the eyes - opened wide.

- You see yourself from the outside (like on a screen in a cinema) and in full length. You see yourself in motion, in the dynamics of the situation, and not in a frozen static picture. It should look like a very short promotional video.

- You see everything brightly, in 3D format, the picture is sensory: filled with pleasant sensations.

- You 100% like everything you see in the visualization. You clearly see yourself as you want to see yourself, doing what you want to do, having important skills, abilities, surrounded by people you want to be surrounded by, and in a situation in which you dream of being.

P. S. Address inspiration from visualization to achieving goals. According to psychologist Gabriel Oettingen, "a positive attitude sometimes leads to negative results." Of course, it's great to believe that "nothing is impossible, the main thing is to think positively," but it's strange to believe that this is enough to change the situation in reality for the better. If you are aware of the obstacles on the way to the goal, and at the same time you are not sad, but act on the basis of today's possibilities, you will achieve more than air-mongers and lazy dreamers or, conversely, inveterate pessimists.

Coach exercise "Life values"

Mark how important each value is for you from 1 to 1.

All your values marked "10" are your "WHY?", your "unfed dragons", real sources for motivation and goals. Sort your "values marked 10" into 4 categories of harmony in life. Choose the most important one in each category. The ability to harmoniously satisfy your true needs and values on your own, or to be able to ask for them calmly - this is your recipe for well-being and confidence. Do not strive for an eternal feeling of happiness and carelessness, strive for a feeling of well-being and harmony in life.

To know your needs + the ability to satisfy them = to be content with your life

Look, what values you have in the "Relationship" area. Choose 3-4 values that are the most important for you, prioritize. Describe them.

Value ... for me it is ...
Value ... for me it is ...
Value ... for me it is ...
Value ... for me it is ...

Abundance		Happiness		Sex	
Achievement		Happiness of others		Sincerity	
Adventures		Harmony		Spirituality	
Beauty		Health		Stability	
Benevolence		Honesty		Success	
Body		Humour		To be the best	
Bravery		Independence		Usefulness	
Calm		Influence		Victory	
Care		Innocence		Wealth	
Career		Inspiration		Well-being	
Celebrity		Interest		Wisdom	
Children		Intelligence		Youth	
Clarity		Intimacy			
Comfort		Joy			
Communication		Justice			
Confidence		Kindness			
Courage		Knowledge			
Creativity		Leadership			
Delight		Liberty			
Development		Lightness			

Discipline	Logic				
Education	Love				
Efficiency	Luxuriance				
Efforts	Money				
Energy	Naivete				
Enjoyment	Optimism				
Entertainment	Orderliness				
Experience	Popularity				
Faith	Possibility				
Family	Power				
Fashion	Practicality				
Fidelity	Procreation				
Firmness	Progress				
Force	Recognition				
Friendship	Respect				
Game	Rest				
Glory	Risk				
Good order	Safety				
Governance	Self-determination				

Relationship	Happiness
The soul is important. I am loved!	Business is important. I'm successful!
Game is important. I am happy!	The body is important. I am beautiful.
Success	Beauty

True worthwhile goals always bring you closer to realizing your values. Note also what is important for your partner, because happy love is a successful exchange of values!

Love your dreams! Concentrate on goals!

You should definitely know what you are striving for. Firstly, in order not to "use a steam-hammer to crack nuts", and secondly, so that an inner core of self-confidence appears. That person is successful who manages to live the way he wants. It means that he has found ground under his feet, he is stable, and he is a reliable support for another person in this changing and unstable world. Those who believe that they control and manage their lives feel more successful, happier, and physically stronger, they live longer.

Dreams and goals are different things. Dreams and desires belong to the sphere of feelings and sensations, these are your "I want!", what is important for you (values). And goals belong to the sphere of activity, and this is the specifics and the plan of action. And the defining question here is the following: "Is it working or not?" We easily and with pleasure do what is working for us. Experience is important here, and it is known to be achieved through training. A feasible dream with a date is already a goal. A goal differs from a dream in the obligatory presence of numbers (dates, criteria for resources, and results). There can be many desires at the same time, large and small, and the goal is a single direction, and it should be clear and specific.

MINUTE OF WISDOM
There is nothing sadder than the lives of women who only knew how to be beautiful.
Bernard Fontenelle, French writer and scientist

How to be effective

Difficult goals should be split into feasible tasks, and then everything becomes possible. If you are not yet sure that you can achieve your goal on time, give yourself more time. Do not give up your goal because of the complexity, but split large tasks into smaller ones that will be feasible for you.

Do not be afraid that it will not work. Try it! The embodiment of your wildest desires is usually at the door marked "Fear". A person cannot be afraid and act at the same time. Take action, the anxiety will go away, and you will feel a surge of energy and inspiration.

Manage your goal! "If we do not manage our goals, then someone else is managing them. Note, not no one, but someone else. It is worth considering, "says psychologist Aleksei Sitnikov. Having a flexible plan for achieving a goal will help you not to abandon it at the first challenge, but to try to achieve it in the best ways for yourself.

The goal can be internal and external. Internal change is always more difficult, but often a person needs to change as an individual to feel happier.

Enjoy the process! Only goals that bring pleasure in the process end in satisfaction. There is no "paradise after the finish line". You have only "here" and "now", and this is your only life.

Take your attention as money and direct it only to what is really important for you. Don't waste it on unnecessary things.

Don't talk about your intentions. Professor Gollwitzer believes that talking about our intentions gives us a "premature sense of completeness." There are so-called "identity symbols" in our brains that help us to form an idea of ourselves. For such a symbol to appear, it is enough not only actions but also just talking about them. For example, if you talk about your desire to write a dissertation, you automatically introduce yourself as a candidate or doctor of science. The brain is satisfied with this play of the imagination, and you lose the motivation to do something to achieve this goal.

Don't make too long task lists. Every day select 3 main actions that bring you closer to the goal, and concentrate on them. Research made by academics Amy Dalton and Steven Spiller shows that cluttering up a task list with too many points causes anxiety, and anxiety steals our strength.

Detail your tasks. Do not write too general phrases, think over the details of the task. Task lists are only harmful if we don't think over the details. In science, there is such a concept - "analysis paralysis" (information overload). It occurs when too long and versatile thinking about a task leads to the fact that working memory "turns off", taking with it that part of the brain that is responsible for willpower - the prefrontal cortex. So that this does not happen, and laziness does not attack, start thinking about the upcoming affair as a series of small and easy tasks for you, each of which will be processed by your brain sequentially, without introducing you into the temptation of procrastination.

Make lists of tasks completed during the day. In such a way you can stimulate your motivation, feel more productive, and notice your accomplishments without missing out. In the evening, write down on the task list what you did not plan to do, but are proud of what you did.

Set tighter deadlines. Rearrange the deadlines for completing tasks to an earlier time - it will allow you not to discourage, but to be more self-disciplined, concentrated, and organized.

Cheer yourself up. Praise yourself for decisiveness and effort, not just for results. The action must be positively reinforced (at least mentally) 3 times: at the time of making a decision, in the process, and immediately after the implementation of the plan.

People are happier when they are busy, idleness makes us feel impatient and unhappy. Don't dawdle, indolence kills the fighting spirit. **During the implementation of the plan, be guided by your own story of the vision of the future.** A person constantly tells himself stories about his life. Create a legend of your life, a beautiful story about an inspiring future: bright, optimistic, based on ideas and life values that lead to the fulfillment of your cherished desires. Remind yourself constantly of the causes and desired consequences, vividly imagine the result, realize the importance of any action that brings you closer to your dreams.

Be decisive. To decide means to act!

Coach exercise "PERFECT GOAL Test (Ideal Goal)"

Write down your goal! When we write down our goals, we formulate them as clearly as possible. A correctly formulated and written goal is already half the battle. Only correctly formulated desires come true easily.

Think about what you want. Write down your goal as intent and test upon seven criteria.

I decided...

P - positive. The goal is stated in the affirmative, in the present tense and in the first person, without particles "not", imperfective verbs, words "want", "need", "must"?

Yes/ No

E - esthetic. Do you vividly visualize the delightful picture of the moment of success, the results that you admire?

Yes/ No

R - real. Are you sure that the achievement of this goal depends on you at least 80% (the remaining 20% you trust in the hands of fate), and you have the necessary external resources and personality traits to achieve the goal?

Yes/ No

F - frank. Is the goal important for you and does it help you to realize your core values in life?

Yes/ No

E - ecological. The goal will not bring harm, but will bring benefit and happiness to you and to the people important for you?

Yes/ No

C - concrete. Is the goal not a condition for the fulfillment of other desires? Is it one, and the plan of the first steps is spelled out?

Yes/ No

T - tasty. Do you want this goal very much, and it makes you want to act immediately?

Yes/ No

If you answered "Yes" seven times, your goal is formulated correctly.

What 3 qualities you should strengthen in yourself to achieve this goal?

LESSON 2

DECIDE WHO YOU WANT TO BECOME.
AND BECOME!

Women are looking for an answer to the question: what should I be to make others fall head over heels in love with me? Or: why do they fall in love with others, but not with me? Is there a bit of universal advice on what you need to be so that the opposite sex loses its head? The answer is - be real! Find your own style of seduction, inherent in you, and bring it to perfection. An image in which your strongest sides will be involved and in which it will feel easy and comfortable.

We are what we think of ourselves. We are everything that arises in our thoughts. With our thoughts, we create ourselves and the world around.

To be or to seem?

Many people suffer from a lack of love: they either do not fall in love themselves or do not know how to make fall in love. It is especially a pity when two ideally suitable persons meet, and the relationship does not work out: the "chemistry", the so-called attraction, was just a little lacking. They failed to fall in love with each other.

How to become a woman who makes easily fall in love?

1. Be inspired!
You definitely need to know what you really want.

Firstly, in order not to "use a steam-hammer to crack nuts", and secondly, so that an inner core of self-confidence appears. That person is successful who manages to live the way he wants. It means that he has found ground under his feet, he is stable, and he is a sweet haven in this changing and unstable world.

INFORMATION FOR REFLECTION

Erich Fromm believed that love is full of meaning only when it does not interfere with full self-expression. Fromm defined love as "a union in which the integrity and individuality of a person are preserved", and noted that the paradox of love is that two people, "becoming united body, still remain two different people."

2. Be attractive!

Both externally and internally, for yourself, and for people. First of all, for yourself. When you like yourself, others feel it and also take a liking to you, at least. A smart appearance is what is noticed first, and this is what will make others want to approach you, or vice versa - move away from you.

The brain works literally - either to approach or to remove: profit or fear, desire, or disgust. Make sure that you make others want to come closer, to listen, to smell, to touch, to kiss ...

3. Be radiant!

Radiance is what shines from within you because all living things in nature strain towards the light. And you are as radiant as your thoughts are.

It is impossible to be a bright person if there are no radiant thoughts. Try to analyze your usual thoughts and cleanse the inner space of those thought viruses that prevent you from achieving success.

You can do it with a simple exercise: set a reminder for every half hour and write down what you are thinking at that moment and what you have been thinking for the last 3 minutes. Analyze - take away the excess.

4. Be sincere!

Showing your real feelings, real emotions is a luxury for a modern person. Instead, there is an opinion that in a relationship you need to endure, try, pretend that everything is fine, look for compromises that supposedly preserve the relationship.

In fact, all of these tricks create imbalance and build-up of tension. From time to time a "release" in the form of scandals, depressions, neurosis, general dissatisfaction with oneself, and a partner, and the world around takes place. This is the price we pay for suppressed feelings and emotions, for hypocrisy, manipulations, and the desire to please, "to be good" at any cost. People who allow themselves to follow their own desires, say what they think, and do what they want, are valuable and attractive, like anything rare in this world.

SMILE
A woman in stockings will never be told: "Dumplings are oversalted."
They will be eaten even if she forgot to cook them.

5. Be unusual!

Falling in love is when we concentrate on someone when we are interested in a person so much that the world around us pales in comparison with him. Love is an emotion that includes a lot of surprise, admiration, "wow" effects.

Remember the men you were in love with - they have always been special for you. And your task is to find and develop "zest" in yourself, to be an interesting, memorable person with whom others are not bored.

Answer yourself - "What is so unusual about me? How do I differ from thousands of other smart and beautiful people? " Start researching yourself, and you will suddenly realize that you scramble eggs in an unusual way or think outside the box, you have some original ideas and talents.

Your signature dishes, travels, life experiences, opinions about films, books, events - it's all you, that's why you are unique.

Becoming a love magnet is a very delightful prospect and a worthy goal. There is no better incentive for personal growth than a loved one next to you, for whose sake you want to become better. But even if he is not next to you yet - become such a person for yourself, to begin with.

Love yourself in practice. Start doing things that will strengthen and develop necessary qualities, and love will surely knock on your door. And you will just have to accept it with the open heart of a self-confident person.

SMILE

A man is capable of any meanness in order to get a girl into bed. Only a woman who has firmly decided to get married can surpass him in this.

Coach exercise "Love yourself!"

I recommend a very good technique that will allow you to explore your selfhood. Take a blank piece of paper and write one of your positive characteristics, for example: "I am well-disposed." And all day try to be kind to people, each time noting this quality in yourself and praising yourself for it. The next day, add something new about your precious self and again "play" "this" all day ... Read the list every day and add your good qualities to it. Duration - 21 days. You can hang this list on the refrigerator. Trust me, you'll learn to focus on the good things in you, and very soon you'll hear compliments about how wonderful you are.

How to rewrite the scenario of personal happiness and stop going "romantic rowing"?

Each of us has her own story, her own episodes and short films of our memory, conscious or unconscious, and they program the course of the history of our life.

They are full of impressions, thoughts, sensations. Someone's life is like a boring TV series, someone's - like an action-packed thriller, or a light comedy, or a sweet and sour melodrama ... The stylistics of our thinking determines the plotline of our story. It is our personal faith.

Our destiny is formed by what we believe in, and who we think we are

It is on our beliefs, on the principles of "what is good, how is it right, how it should be" the stories that we tell about ourselves, about men, about people, and about life, in general, are formed. These stories-beliefs keep senses from our distant childhood. And senses give us strength for new achievements or take our energy away.

Hence the answer to the question: will we have enough strength for changes, or will we "skip out" on all our goals and dreams? If there is a sense (a coincidence with our deepest beliefs, values) - we do, if there is no sense - we feign excuses for ourselves.

The main storyline, the leading story of destiny, a fairy tale about ourselves, in which we firmly believe all our lives, was told to us by our parents.

In the period from 3 to 6 years, the seed of the story "My destiny" is formed, it is then that a person answers the most important question for himself, "Who am I?", and further on everything depends on the quality of the ground where the seed gets, whether it is fertile or arid and desert. But mostly everything depends on the quality of the core, whether there is enough or not enough strength for growth and prosperity.

For us little ones, our parents were gods, the most important providers of happiness or misfortune, severe judges, and dear guardian angels. Their reaction to our actions, their indirect suggestion of what was good and what was bad, created our identity.

During all life, the sense of justice instilled by parents will determine the emotional background of our lives.

We believe that what is happening and what we are doing is "Good!" (which means it's right), "I'm a good girl," we rejoice, "Not good. Bad girl"- we grieve.

And until we deal with ourselves and realize these principles, instead of constantly trying to suppress our feelings, resist them, we will follow our childish convictions, like rats follow a magic pipe.

Not but that our parents are bad people or want to teach us anything that gets in the way of our happiness. No! They simply told and/or showed us their principles of life, which helped them adapt to reality. THEIR reality! Taking into account THEIR personal characteristics and THEIR life circumstances.

And if you fully consider THEIR example of life to be acceptable and desirable, and if the results of your life completely satisfy you, and you live the life you dream about, then welcome to the childhood fairy tale! And if not, then you live the life that you deserve, or rather, the one that you have formed yourself within you. Or the one that your parents formed for you in your distant childhood.

We have grown up and now clearly realize that our parents are ordinary people with their own advantages and disadvantages, their own worldview, which we like or dislike. But childish stories still define our reality …

For every woman, dad is the navigator of her femininity, mom is the mirror of her femininity. If we liked the way our mother behaved and looked, we try to copy her, if we did not like our mother's life, we try to turn away and become her complete opposite.

Mom forms the outer shell of femininity, dad forms the inner component.

And also the core of femininity, our inner man. The core of self-confidence as a woman, that you deserve to love and be loved, that you can be adored unconditionally.

All girls who have received enough love from their dad consider themselves magical princesses for life, accepting the worship of princes of all stripes and kingdoms.

You never stop being a little Daughter for your dad! And for the men around you, your confidence becomes a magnet, a force that they are trying to possess, an energy that they want to feed on.

We always try to get from communication with men what we did not receive from our mother.

The discoveries of British scientists are interesting. They surveyed prostitutes and found that almost all "priestesses of love" choose this profession at the need of the heart, and not because of hopelessness, and enjoy the profession.

It has emerged that 98% of them are women "not cared for enough" by mothers, who have received less attention, hugs, kisses, motherly warmth from their mothers in childhood.

Perhaps, a long time ago in childhood, your mother was not hugged, embraced by her mother, or she had other things to worry about. A sort of generic karma.

By the way, this is how the "fate of the family", all sorts of "celibacy wreath" and other heresies are formed. The grown-up girl just repeats her mother's mistakes as the only sure way to survive in the world of men. Well, the results in personal life copy the mother's fate.

SMILE

Medicine news. German scientists have created the drug "Antiviagra" for a calm and thoughtful viewing of porn films.

INFORMATION FOR REFLECTION

Once Sir Francis Galton (one of the most prominent figures in the history of world psychology) decided on a kind of experiment. Before going on a daily stroll through the streets of London, he instilled himself: "I am a disgusting person hated by everyone in England!" Galton concentrated on this conviction for several minutes, it was tantamount to self-hypnosis, and went, as usual, to the promenade.

However, it only seemed that everything was as usual. In fact, the following happened. At every step, Francis caught the contemptuous and disgusting glances of passers-by. Many people turned away from him, several times rude abuse sounded in his address.

In the port, one of the movers, when Galton passed him, kicked the scientist with his elbow so that he flopped into the mud. It seemed that hostility was passed on even to the animals. When he passed the harnessed stallion, it kicked the scientist in the thigh so that he fell to the ground again. Galton tried to evoke sympathy from eyewitnesses, but, to his amazement, he heard that people began to protect the animal.

Galton hurried home, not waiting for his thought experiment to lead to more serious consequences.

This true story is described in many psychology textbooks. Two important conclusions can be drawn from it.

1. A person is what he thinks of himself.

2. There is no need to inform others about your self-esteem and state of mind. They will feel it anyway.

SMILE
- Faina Yakovlevna, how would you describe your life in a few words?
- For what?!

How to get rid of negative programs?

To grow up! It means that you should stop being your mother's little daughter (to become first her friend, and then her mother) and realize those childish principles that are now guiding your life, to lead your feelings. Do not follow thoughtlessly your once formed beliefs, but realize them, revise and change them for those that bring you closer to female happiness, and do not lead you into childish reflections.

Coach exercise "Message from childhood"

Write what negative things people who are important for you said about you in childhood. Mother? Father?

How did it affect your destiny? Do these beliefs bring you closer to your dreams? Do they help you? Do you agree with them?

What image of yourself do you choose? What kind of person are you really? What personality traits are you proud of? How will they help you in achieving your life goals?

Take an unbiased look at your potential

Every woman wants to be attractive and even very attractive. And from time to time each of us is overtaken by minutes of painful thoughts about our person. We often doubt. Sometimes we doubt the adequacy of men - "they do not notice such a clever beauty like me." Sometimes we doubt ourselves - "Am I really so beautiful if when I appear on the streets of the city the traffic is not blocked because of the chaos caused by crowds of fans?" And what do they, men, it should seem, want from you? What do they miss? Why don't they besiege you with text messages and flowers at night?

Try, casting aside a false shame and invoking all your prudence, to answer the question: "And, really, why?"

First, go to a mirror that reflects you in full growth - it will tell the truth better than any well-intentioned friend. If you were a man, would this girl attract you? By what? Look into her eyes first. Do they have a calm, steady light of confidence and harmony with themselves? Do these eyes sparkle with joy and mischief? Is the look soft and tender?

Do you want to trust the person in the mirror? Look at your posture, straighten your shoulders.

Now check out this girl's style. Can you call her feminine? What is she wearing? How is she brushed-up? Does she have cared-for look? Note in your appearance 3-10 primary advantages: from an incredibly beautiful earlobe to the figure of a top model. These will be your advantages, pride, and investment. For example, naturally beautiful hair needs decent care - do not skimp on hair shine and expensive cosmetics for it. Decorate your graceful wrists with bracelets, delicate aristocratic fingers with refined rings. The basic principle is to focus on your attractive features, thereby distracting from the unattractive ones. Trying to think about your advantages, you will soon begin to notice that people around you also see only positive in you.

Remember: thought is material, and you are able to infect people with your thought-forms. It's not difficult to improve your appearance: a couple of kilograms off, a good stylist and make-up artist - you are beautiful. But as for the look and the smile, things are more complicated. For kindness and tenderness in the look, for a radiant ingenuous smile, cosmetics cannot be bought even in the most glamorous salons and boutiques. The look translates your thoughts to others.

By the way, what do you think people want you to think about in their presence? About them, of course! And to think well about them. And if this is a man, believe me, he wants to impress, he really wants to delight you with himself!

To impress others, try to make them impress you. Create the conditions under which the man will open up: sincerely ask him about himself and his interests, opinions on this or that point. Notice the good and you will get a mutual interest in return.

Remember: **of all women, a man will choose the most cheerful first. Of the cheerful - the most beautiful. Of the beautiful - the wisest.** Develop in this direction: learn to be cheerful, improve your appearance, and do not stop learning. Now there is a lot of literature on psychology and relationships - study it, become smarter, more interesting, first of all, for yourself. Believe me: it is not at all difficult to please others when you become the one who likes yourself. Before you attract the perfect man, become a magnet for him - judge what exactly should attract him. Remember the all-pervading principle of the Universe: like seeks like. It means, first of all, people with the same quality of thoughts are attracted. If you want to meet a confident man, start thinking, acting, and living according to the principles of a successful woman. At first, it is enough to just pretend to be like that, and then ... If you believe - others will believe as well! Do you want a millionaire husband? Start thinking well of yourself and convince yourself that you deserve the best in this life.

If a woman is determined to become happy, she will certainly face a change. You will have to change. But the goal is worth it. Just imagine the admiring, loving glance of the future chosen one! Have you imagined it? Then forward to a new future!

Beckon, attract, enchant!

SMILE

Women's reason.

- Firstly, I didn't take anything!

- Secondly, I have already put back.

MINUTE OF WISDOM

If a woman shows her mettle, they say about her - a cantankerous woman. If a man shows his mettle, they say about him - he is a good guy.

Margaret Thatcher

Coach exercise "Assessment of the level of female magnetism"

List your attractive features. What you are proud of, what you love in yourself: appearance, character, knowledge, abilities. In the second column write down your disadvantages using the same principle.

What I like about myself	What I don't like about myself

Take a look at the result and imagine that the second column is a list of cons of your best friend, who, as you think, definitely underestimates herself. Choose from it the points that you are ready to forgive and accept. Now cross them out. Further, choose those disadvantages that can be minimized. Write a plan to correct each of these features. With the others, you just have to come to terms, not to talk about them and not to demonstrate to others, but it is better to forget about these features altogether, well, at least for a while. It is better to focus on your positive qualities and on the plan of action.

And start treating yourself as a friend, as your closest and beloved friend. Inspire yourself and change.

A step-by-step strategy for achieving personal happiness

You want to get married, you dream of love, but no one proposes marriage. You feel sad. I understand you, your bad mood is justified, this is really a tragedy, a reason to sigh a little with your friends.

But only for an ordinary girl! And if you are a purposeful girl, and I suspect that you are, since you are reading this book, then I congratulate you! A new interesting and exciting challenge has appeared in your life. And it's time to rethink your approach to solving problems in your personal life. You need to look at reality with your beautiful, painted eyes and take responsibility for your fate into your own hands. "Better be born ambitious than rich. Take action!" - reads one of the rules of LoveQ-coaching, although, of course, good looks have not discouraged anyone yet.

I ask you to excuse me in advance for the directness and the presence of non-romantic vocabulary - I want to offer a new, business-like approach to solving problems in personal life.

And let's start with getting rid of illusions - this is the first and necessary step to any change. Let's be honest. Men that you like are often not single, there is some kind of muse nearby. It's just not you. So it's time to think - why?

The answer is banal: they do not like you or you do not fall into their field of vision. All other assumptions are self-deception. And if you prefer to live in illusions, then stop reading and go back to your girlfriends. They "will both understand and support."

I will not befog your consciousness - after all, you will have to pay for it with loneliness in old age.

And this is a too high price for a good girl.

All beautiful things should be paired! Each of us deserves love - you just sometimes need to reconsider your beliefs and re-approach your personal life in a businesslike manner.

Sometimes asking yourself the right questions on time can improve your life. It's time to take a serious approach to success in your personal life. Try to solve the issue not emotionally, but rationally, making your own plan of personal happiness. Maybe it will work out!

I advise you to answer the questions in written form.

SMILE
- Well, why are you looking at me like that?
- I'm trying to understand what I have found in you.
- What others have lost!

SMILE
Two friends are talking:
- Sasha, what would you say if you met a kind, affectionate, gentle woman who would forgive everything and cook well?
Sasha, having thought:
- Hello, mom...

STEP 1. Analysis of the current situation

Describe your personal life situation in three sentences.

Who are you as a woman? Describe yourself in five sentences. What real (and not imposed by slick magazines) needs do you have?

Remember, what difficulties did you face last year? Make a list and you will understand your life tasks (needs).

Looking at the entire list, answer the question: "What one word can denote the entire list?" This is your basic need at the moment.

STEP 2. Goal setting

I understand that in personal life it is customary to rely on fate, but we have agreed to approach the issue in a new way.

So, let's make a goal out of the dream of personal happiness. A goal differs from a dream in realism, specificity, and the presence of an implementation plan.

For happiness in love, you need a partner. Your goal is to meet and interest the right man in your persona.

You should decide on all the criteria.

What is personal happiness for you? How is it interconnected with your global life plans in all areas? What kind of man do you need? To the maximum? To the minimum? Who is he? What is he?

We define the criteria: geographical, social, psychophysical characteristics of the target audience. Where are the men of your dreams? What do they live and breathe with? Where, when, how, and why are you ready to meet your betrothed?

STEP 3. Market analysis

It is an assessment of reality and competition in the marriage market.

What kind of woman is the man of your dreams interested in? Write down 20 characteristics. Highlight 4 the most important for you. What these women are distinct from you in?

STEP 4. Brand analysis

You are a brand named after yourself. And let me assume that there is a high probability that it (your brand) is not in demand among the target audience (the men you dream of). Sorry, but this is also a great personal growth path for you.

Relate reality to desires.

Let us find out what values and needs the target audience has, and begin work on their acceptance and compliance. How will you be useful and interesting for them? How will you hook?

Assess your strengths and weaknesses objectively - these are internal evaluation criteria, i.e. what you are able to influence.

Assess the opportunities and threats of the situation in which you are - these are the factors of the outside environment (and here you cannot always influence, but only accept as a given).

It is important to assess the risks - and this is a competitive environment. To do this, remember the women that the men of your dreams like. What are the advantages of these women? What can they do that you can not do? What are the disadvantages of these women? What are your advantages? What skills do you need to hone? What information, knowledge is not enough? What qualities in yourself do you need to develop? And how?

If necessary, we rely on a romantic rebranding or, I beg your pardon, lower the request level.

SMILE

- Well, I go along the street, so beautiful, and all the guys I meet just petrify, and those who are weaker - just fall, fall, fall and stack themselves!
From the movie "Girls"

STEP 5. Development of a set of plans to achieve the goal

Think over a brand promotion plan (promotion of yourself) for your target group. It is a step-by-step strategy with a timeline and detailed description in financial and marketing terms, with dates and criteria for the result assessment.

What will you do? What are the 4 important points of your plan? It is better to sketch out several variants - the main one and several alternative variants.

Think over a strategy for each, i.e. what and how you will do if everything goes according to plan, as well as crisis strategies. Hope for the best, but prepare for the worst. Make your bets not on one admirer, but on several. A woman should have a choice!

By the way, it will help not to fall into excessive emotionality and overthinking.

STEP 6. Resources raising

To achieve the goal, you will need financial and time resources. Wardrobe, makeup, figure, trips, courses, seminars - the minimum that will require investment at the first stage.

By the way, no business plan is accepted immediately. The investor, as a rule, considers possible variants and then asks to cut down expenses. Think about the economical variant at once. Develop a creative approach to problem solving.

STEP 7. Plan Implementation

Pursue your agenda, but be flexible. If you don't like the situation, change your strategy, and possibly your plan.

Remember, if you play your game, a positive result is inevitable!
INFORMATION FOR REFLECTION
Basic beliefs of a happy woman

1. *The universe is abundant! Therefore, the world has everything I need.*
2. *All the time in the world belongs to me! Therefore, I choose without fuss, try, calmly, and confidently go to the goal.*
3. *The main thing is the process, not the result! Therefore, I will enjoy the process of achieving the goal.*
4. *I am proud of myself! Therefore, others admire me.*
5. *I am the most important person in the world for myself! Therefore, my desires, needs, ideas, decisions are important and paramount.*
6. *I am the mistress of my life! Therefore, only I decide how to live.*

*7. **Everything is possible!** Therefore, I will act in the best way for me.*

*8. **I am the best expert in my life!** Therefore, I am guided by my own criteria for assessing myself and allow myself to make mistakes.*

Create your personal brand!

In a narrow sense, a brand is your reputation, the impression you make on others. A brand is not only your actions. It is also based on your strengths, human and professional qualities, talents and skills, attitude towards family, friends, and life in general.

Branding is a great tool for self-development and self-motivation. You study yourself and create your own "message", come up with a strategy of behavior and brand promotion called "I". Developing and promoting your brand can go a long way toward propelling you towards happiness in your personal life.

You need to study yourself. You need to understand your beliefs, your strengths, and realize what message you are sending to others. Identify your resource, figure out where improvements are needed to live the life you deserve. A personal brand helps you choose the right vector and follow it. Adequacy and systematic actions are important here. Behavioral flexibility is also very important. Monitor: if a behavior strategy does not work, then change it to a more effective one.

A personal brand is a message that you convey to the world. A personal brand doesn't exist without an audience, it always works for someone. In your personal life, it is aimed at the category of men who meet the qualities of your potential beloved.

MINUTE OF WISDOM

There is not much difference between a million and a billion dollars - oysters do not become tastier.

Andrey Andreev, founder of Badoo

Coach exercise "I am a brand"

Answer the questions that will help you analyze your brand.

What am I as a woman?...

…as an individual?

_____

What is my specialness?

_____

How am I different from my competitors?

_____

What do I want others to think of me?

_____

How will they understand that I am like this?

_____

What are my obvious disadvantages?

_____

What is my plan for self-improvement?

_____

What are the simplest first steps I am ready to take in the coming week?

_____

Coach exercise "Portrait of an ideal partner"

Sit down, take a piece of paper and try to describe the Man of your Dreams (M) as accurately as possible, as if you are making an order from the Universe, in four categories.

1. His anatomical and physical characteristics.

Appearance, height, weight, health condition, sexual potential, food preferences, attitude towards sports, mode of dress, etc.

_____

_____

2. His character.

Temperament, relations with friends. Positive features, some negative ones, etc.

_____

_____

3. His social status.

Profession, financial situation, attitude towards money. Hobby, preferred type of leisure, interests, etc.

_____

_____

4. His attitude towards you.

_____

_____

5. How should he show feelings so that you feel that you are desired and loved?

_____

_____

6. What does he value and love in you, what is he ready for for you? Jealousy, gifts, tenderness?

_____

_____

7. What will you enjoy doing together, what traditions will you have?

_____

_____

8. What should he do in relation to you and what should he never do?

_____

_____

9. If you have a tiff, how should he make amends?

_____

_____

10. His attitude towards the family, children.

_____

_____

11. Why does he need this relationship at all?

_____

_____

Looking at this description, make a list of 10 the most important criteria for your future chosen one. Who and what kind of person should he be to be the man whose love you dream of?

1._____
2._____
3._____
4._____
5._____
6._____
7._____
8._____
9._____
10._____

Now use your imagination and visualize the image of a man (the one that came to your mind in the first seconds) to each of the characteristics separately. First, imagine a man who has a quality number 1. And make this quality somewhat exaggerated, bright, and the others - secondary and unexpressed. For example, you wrote "generous". So, visualize in your imagination a person who is incredibly generous, but not too rich and beautiful. Then put a number in front of each characteristic of a man - the degree of importance for you of this quality according to a ten-point scale. When evaluating, rely on your inner feelings that arose when you fantasized.

We choose a partner with our hearts, and the degree of satisfaction with the relationship will depend on our internal, often unconscious ideas and images. Now make a list of 10 characteristics of the future partner that scored the highest rating. Enter them in the left column.

And, having thought logically, write down in the right column the female characteristics corresponding to each item separately. In other words, make a list of the qualities that should be inherent in the woman of his dreams - the one that can captivate, to be necessary and interesting for him.

For example, if you wrote "handsome" on the left, write "pretty" on the right. He is a "gourmet" - she is "a great cook." Is he interested in golf? It means that he will be interested in a girl who is also interested in golf or knows how to keep up a conversation on this topic, etc.

Be guided by logic, do not forget about the principle of mutually beneficial exchange and complementary abilities. After that, put in front of each female characteristic a score from one to ten, depending on how much this quality is inherent in you personally. Only, mind, honestly.

Characteristics of MAN of DREAMS	Characteristics of WOMAN of DREAMS	My score

Here you have a plan for self-improvement. And before you start working on yourself and look for a young man who meets all your needs, read the room.

Do such men exist in nature and how often are they found?

A Dream Man should be turned into a Goal Man for him to *be attainable.* Look at the list once again. Our desires, often dictated by stereotypes of society, are contradictory in nature and unlimited in content. We want everything at once. But it is not realistic. Determine your priorities, understand what you need. Being an adequate girl, decide for yourself: either you will make every effort to "self-tuning", or lower your needs. And it is very probable that by listening to yourself, you will understand that you can be happy and not with a superman, but with an earthly man with whom you are united by common interests, values, dreams. After all, you can grow together and create the future you dream of. Perhaps it is thanks to you that he will turn into a Dream Man.

Refer to your experience - remember your past relations.

What did you like and what did you dislike about a man?

_____

_____

What was missing in your relationship?

_____

_____

How did your partners fit the description of the man of your dreams?

_____

_____

Why did you choose this partner then?

_____

_____

When and why were you happy with him?

_____

_____

What are your real, not imagined, needs?

_____

_____

Maybe in the end you will want to correct the list - do it.
Coach exercise "Man - Goal"

Who is He?

_____

What is He?

_____

What does he do?

_____

What problems and needs does this category of men have?

_____

What kind of women are usually interesting and useful to such men?

_____

Why?

_____

_____

What skills and abilities are necessary to become more attractive for this category of men?

_____

_____

How can I be interesting and useful for such men?

_____

_____

What can I do for this?

_____

_____

What special do you give him that other women do not give him?

_____

What will you give in marriage that you don't give now?

Change the requirements to yourself. Begin to turn into a Woman of Dream for your future beloved from tomorrow. Before you manage your dream, learn to manage yourself.

Make a daily plan of 3-5 specific actions: diet, sports, change in style, new knowledge, habits ... Happiness in your personal life is a huge victory, which consists of small daily victories.

And also - be patient. **Patience is the greatest wisdom**. The search for the man of your dreams should bring pleasure and inspire you to become better, so that one day when you meet, he does not pass by, but wants to be your loved one at all costs and make you happy.

SMILE

Family psychologists advise, when you are late coming home, tell your wife something like: "You look amazing today!" And if you entered the apartment on all fours, and cannot raise your head, you can praise her pedicure. And if you don't have the strength to speak at all, you can lick her leg and whimper softly.

Coach exercise "Where can the men be found?"

Answer: *EVERYWHERE! IT'S IMPORTANT TO MAKE THE ACQUAINTANCE!*

Understanding what he is - the man of your dreams, ask yourself: where can such men be found? Write a list of 10 the most potential places - search there, what is more, search regularly.

Who is my potential Man of Dreams?

In which audience of men can he be attributed?

What does he do?

What does he like?

How does he take rest?

Where are these people: physically and online, so that I can reach them?

How can I be heard and seen by members of my audience? How and with what will I draw their attention to me?

Where can we meet and communicate with them?

What is my plan for active systematic actions?

What are the simplest first steps I am ready to take in the coming week?

SMILE

At the courses of men seduction:
- Today we'll talk about lace lingerie ...
- And if we have no money for lace lingerie?
- Then we take the usual panties, fold them into five, take the scissors ...
And now we remember how we made paper snowflakes in childhood ...

How to Marry a Successful Man?

Once I asked my friend from Switzerland, a very successful businessman, a millionaire, eligible bachelor: "What is the main advice you can give to girls who dream of winning the heart of a man like you?" **He pondered for a minute and replied, "Don't put a man in the center of the universe!"**

I was surprised at his advice and was convinced of my supposal about the main mistake of the women "gold diggers". Many of them try so hard to please a man that they completely forget about themselves, about their plans in life, and direct all their energy to being in the right place at the right time and looking stunning. This, of course, is the correct active approach of a modern girl. I am deeply convinced that active people win in our world. But you need to start your path to happiness in your personal life not with getting around, but with a great desire to please yourself, a respect for yourself. And as a result, to get the life in which you will be happy, and not just rich and married.

Note, I did not say "the life you dream about." Dreams of every second girl are identical and not particularly original, and their fulfillment does not always make her happy. Sometimes money and a husband appear, but there is no feeling of happiness. Because it is quite possible, she achieved social success, but not her own, that could make her happy if she sorted herself out in time.

Successful men know better than anyone that time is money! They do not put relationships first in their lives and therefore allocate their energies wisely. They don't give it away for no reason and immediately. "First of all, the planes, but what about the girls?" And the girls are definitely not First. A woman needs to make an effort to draw attention to herself. Even if you are very beautiful, it is not a fact that he will be interested in you for more than one evening. Although, if you are a brainy girl and you have managed to accept some prestigious title in the beauty industry, then an oligarch husband is almost guaranteed to you. Such titles as well as oligarchs are not numerous and, being snobs, oligarchs are happy to add another trophy to their various achievements.

But while you are not Miss Galaxy yet, you can use Formula 4 C.

Formula 4 C

To be a woman of dreams for a worthy man means to be at the same time:

Courageous — *learn to despise fear!*

Cheerful — *be happy!*

Cute — *be sweet, warm in communication, feminine, but not cloying!*

Classy — *in everything!* Clothes, everyday life, richness of speech, social circle, occupation ... Subtle things do not exist.

I named this formula after the diamond peer review system. Typically, a stone is evaluated according to four parameters 4 "C", where the first "C" means carat weight, the second "C" - color, the third "C" - clarity, the fourth "C" - cut.

Decent men are not used to buying cheap diamonds, in fact, as well as wasting their time on women who do not know their worth.

As Rothschild said: *"I'm not rich so to buy cheap things."* And when purchasing precious stones, they are guided by two important principles.

1. **All is not a diamond that glitters.** When buying a diamond, one must be sober in its choice. And they are very scrupulous about the choice of a spouse!

2. **A good stone will not be sold cheaply.** They definitely pay attention to the parameters of the stone, including the cut. Without a quality cut, the stone will appear dead. Well, if we continue to draw an analogy with the choice of a girl, then you should demonstrate selectivity, self-worth, not jump into bed at a run on the first evening, even if it was spent romantically on a yacht. An impeccable reputation, high self-esteem and a set of vivid bright emotions are desirable. After all, they are often lacking for busy people.

I do not try to level down your ambitions. I just suggest that you objectively evaluate your strengths and first understand yourself and your true desires, so that later there will be no disappointment. Set goals for yourself that will not be aimed at finding a "millionaire" who is obliged to fulfill your dreams, but at finding yourself and your own path to happiness and harmony. I am sure you will definitely meet your Prince along the way.

The way to the man of your dreams is always the way to yourself and the best incentive for self-improvement. And if you decided to take on the road only your beautiful body and hastily learned geisha techniques, then I sympathize with you. Although no! I express my condolences!

If you decide to act, then consider your capabilities and needs, make a plan, and try to do it without a focus on results. Make it your goal - to enjoy your search. For example, enrolling in a golf club or a prestigious sports club is a good idea, but only if you are really going to learn how to play golf and you really enjoy the sport. And if you're just going to sit in a cafe, as if you're hunting in ambush, then you shouldn't. You are likely to be perceived as a one night stand.

Be sure to think about what you will talk about with a man if you still manage to make an acquaintance and make a good impression. Learn to be well versed in wines, hone impeccable manners, and basic knowledge of male psychology and the psychology of wealthy people.

Are you going to lighten your hair because gentlemen prefer blondes? You are welcome to change your hair color if you want to experiment with your look. But if you like yourself more as a brunette - stop!

Do everything with love for yourself, and not to please other people's whims or expectations.

A woman who feels harmony within herself is the most seductive image for men. Even a flawless appearance will not help you to attract a man if you think unattractively. It is very important what mental message you send into space. Our thoughts become our destiny. In order to attract the right man, you need to think in unison with him, to create the right thought forms. **You need to believe that he needs you and only you are able to make your chosen one truly happy.**

SMILE

- Attention, now we will test you for IQ.

- And what is it?

- The test is over.

MINUTE OF WISDOM

Until the final decision is made, you will be tortured by doubts, you will always remember that there is a chance to turn back, and this will not allow you to work effectively. But at the moment when you decide to completely devote yourself to your work, Providence is on your side. Such things begin to happen that could not have happened under other circumstances ... Whatever you are capable of, whatever you dream of, start to materialize it. Courage gives a person strength and even magical power. Take your chance!

Johann Goethe

Marriage of convenience!

It is important to decide what you want more - a man or money? First of all, do you need a man in the house, a father of your future children, a gentle lover, a caring friend or a wallet sticking out of your pants? **My good advice is not to make money a priority.** After all, you will have to fall asleep, and most importantly, wake up with a living person, and not with an ATM in an embrace.

You need to understand what kind of man can make you even happier, who you need. Note, not who you want, but who you need. After all, it happens that a girl picks up such a coveted rich guy, and after a short time she does not feel happy anymore and remembers, and yearns for some Vasya from the next doorway, who may not be rich, but so dear!

People are united by common interests, beliefs, conversations, dreams, values. And money is just an opportunity to enjoy life together. Do not confuse finance with love. You need to look for a person with a certain set of personal qualities, not functions. If he is both strong and purposeful, he will be well-off sooner or later.

Look for a guy with potential, and if you truly love and inspire him, he will definitely become rich. Although, if before the age of 40 a man did not have financial ups, then it is unlikely that he can count on them in the future, even with all your energy and enthusiasm.

And so, if you want to get married of convenience, then first of all, let's count on good human relations. Count on love and understanding. And believe in yourself and the best. And you will definitely meet your soul mate!

INFORMATION OF REFLECTION

Choose the habitat of your target audience.

- *Social media.*
- *Dating sites.*
- *Marriage agencies.*
- *Hiking groups.*
- *Special interest clubs: English etc.*
- *Training courses (men mainly attend business and personality trainings).*
- *Bowling clubs.*
- *Billiard saloons.*
- *Rifle groups.*
- *Showcases.*
- *Business conferences.*
- *Massage, tantra classes.*
- *New groups of friends (you can ask to invite you to general parties).*
- *Automobile dealerships.*
- *Golf-clubs.*
- *Winter sports resorts.*
- *Overseas weekend trips.*
- *Thematic forums (as a rule, on the city portals).*
- *Parks (morning run).*
- *Fitness-clubs , swimming pools.*
- *Cafes, restaurants (especially during business lunch).*
- *Presentation parties.*
- *Photo courses.*
- *"Mafia" game.*
- *Beaches.*
- *Men's clothing stores (you can ask for advice).*
- *Supermarkets (you can ask for help in choosing elite alcohol or ask to bring a bag to the car).*
- *Specialized exhibitions are generally Klondike.*

Your variants:

_____

_____

_____

_____

_____

_____

LESSON 3

FALL IN LOVE WITH YOURSELF! TREAT YOURSELF THE WAY YOU WOULD LIKE YOUR BOYFRIEND TO TREAT YOU!

The attitude of men towards you is always a mirror reflection of your attitude towards yourself! No one can love you truly if you do not love yourself! That is, people will be carried away by you, they will be in sympathy with you, especially if you are an attractive person, but they will not love you for a long time and seriously! Therefore, you need not only to feel sympathy for yourself but to love yourself with unconditional love!

When we love without conditions, we accept a person even with his weaknesses, which seem nice to us. All our thoughts, desires, plans are concentrated on the only one. Each of his actions seems to be correct and significant. Next to him, life is filled with joy, meaning and inspiring plans. This is how you should treat yourself, your life and your dreams! And only then you will not have problems with fans who will seek your love and affection.

Become your superhero! Love yourself for all those who could not appreciate you. Do not think that to love yourself, you need only to want it. No! Falling in love with yourself is like starting life from scratch. You need to make an effort to change - to become self-confident. To become light.

You have a lot to learn:
firstly, to manage yourself;
secondly, to manage your mood;
thirdly, to set goals and achieve them easily.

How to attract love into your life?

We are waiting for a Great Love, which will illuminate our life and fill it with joy and meaning. It seems to us that as soon as Prince Charming appears at the threshold of our hearts, the door will open and a continuous feast of Love and Mutual understanding will begin. We all, like Sleeping Beauties, hope for a magic kiss from the one that will color our gray everyday life with a colorfulness of emotions.

Of course, an expectation of the beautiful is beautiful in itself (sorry for the tautology), and it will happen if you observe the most important law of Love:

"Men fall in love only with a woman who is in love with herself!"

To love yourself means to BECOME YOURSELF! To love your life! To love your dreams! To put yourself in the center of the universe called "My life!" In order to control yourself, you need to control your thoughts. To become a "king in your head", or rather a "Queen".

Until we stop constantly gnawing ourselves on the inside with doubts, we do not feel our inherent value, we have as little chance of seeing Love as of seeing our own ears. Nathaniel Branden writes: *"In order to strive for any good, one must consider oneself worthy of possessing them. In order to fight for your happiness, you need to consider yourself worthy of happiness. "*

Admit to yourself that you have your strengths and weaknesses, and try to present the dark part of your nature to others as a highlight. After all, it is often because of them that people fall in love with us.

Allowing yourself to be nonideal, you thereby recognize the other person's right to be nonideal, and it makes the other person more comfortable next to us. It's important to learn how to hold a supportive internal dialogue. Get rid of thoughts that make you doubt, undermine your self-confidence.

To any haunting thought, say: "Stop!" Or enter into a dialogue with it. Ask it several questions: "Is what I'm thinking about now a fact? Why do I need this thought? What do I really want? " And launch in your mind instead of a negative thought, another, convincing, life-affirming and useful for yourself. Learn to convince yourself - in such a way you will become convincing for others!

Shakespeare wrote very truly: *"There is neither bad nor good, only thought makes things as they seem to us."* Free your brain of mental refuse. Remember how confident, what Perfection you seem to be to yourself next to an admirer who does not interest you - this is exactly how you should behave with a man you want to make fall in love with you. **Adore yourself!** Think well of yourself, idealize yourself, and you will definitely fall in love with yourself and will make others fall in love with you.

To love your life means learning to take pleasure in little things and enjoy the moment. We live like in a spacesuit of emotional stress and worries about the past or the future. But the art of enjoying life lies in the ability to enjoy the moment. To make a man next to you happy, you do not need to try to please him, you need to try to please yourself. Do not fuss, but think about how to enjoy your life here and now.

Life is full of joy! A person is born for happiness as a bird for a flight! Start to notice all the good things that surround you. Become a hedonist and you will become light.

Our plans should inspire us and make our life meaningful. Prioritize correctly: a man should never be your main super goal, the "navel of the universe", otherwise you will quickly lose him. Put personal achievements first, be a purposeful person and notice the smallest successes on the way to success. Reasonable selfishness is essential for personal happiness.

Just decide for yourself that from now on you start behaving like a happy person, thinking as a happy person, living as a happy person, and treating yourself with love. Believe me, then luck will knock on your door. Only a happy person can make someone else happy next to him. Only if you have something you can share it. So love yourself and share your love. And it will certainly return to you multiplied.

MINUTE OF WISDOM
A woman is smarter than a man, and she spends her intellect, first of all, to prevent a man from noticing it.
Mary McCarthy, American writer

MINUTE OF WISDOM
A woman attracts men, playing on her charm, and keeps them close to her, playing on their vices.
Somerset Maugham

Love yourself in deed!

To love yourself correctly means to love yourself objectively and in deed. To make gestures for yourself and to treat yourself with care, to please yourself.

For example, if you love your cat, you don't just tell her that all day. No. You try to do something pleasant and useful for her. You indulge her, and sometimes you punish and scold her so that she is more organized for her own good.

The basis of your actions is taking care of her, of her needs. So you need to love yourself in practice as well.

Become a VIP for yourself - the most important person in the world! All the best is for yourself and about yourself. Start thinking good about yourself. Imagine that you already have ideal qualities. The English say: "Fake it till you make it". Any personality trait is just a skill that you can train if you want. The best way to change yourself is to get into a new role, at first just "playing" it. Following the formula of psychologist William James: "If you want to develop some quality in yourself, behave as if you already have it", you will strengthen the image of the "new Me", you will begin to respect yourself, that means that it will be easier for you to fall in love with yourself.

Live the day playing "as if". Just imagine that you already have your best qualities. And you will not notice yourself how the new characteristics will become a part of the real you.

Start making gestures that will strengthen and develop the necessary qualities, and love will surely knock on your door. And you just have to accept it with the open heart of a self-confident person.

Place yourself in the center of the universe called "My Life".

Live for yourself, realize your desires. You need to work on your self-esteem, understand and know yourself, feel your true desires and look for opportunities to implement them, and not to devalue them.

Compliment yourself. In the evening ask yourself the question: "If today I was praised by a person who is an example for me, what would I hear?" You are worthy of recognition! After all, all the best in your life happen thanks to you.

Concentrate on your strengths and the positive aspects of the situation.

SMILE

Once upon a time, there was a princess who dreamed that one day a handsome prince would come and kiss her ...

Once upon a time, there was a prince who dreamed that one day a beautiful princess would come and kiss him ...

And so these two toads met ...

Turn loneliness into freedom and enjoy it!

Loneliness is a gray word. We talk about it, and the soul becomes slushy and meaningless. It makes us stay at home in the evenings and dream of that wonderful moment when we get rid of it and finally become happy. But it is not all that bad. The deeper the loneliness, the more you strive for happiness, which means that the motivation to change the situation and find love grows. There is an emptiness in the soul, and by filling it, you can feel happier. And people are drawn to happy ones.

There are reasons for mental discomfort, they are the lack of something important. There are five reasons, five types of loneliness and five solutions to this problem.

1. Words. You need an interlocutor and you lack communication, support and encouragement. Of course, after all, a word warmly said gives comfort even to a cat, and even more to a woman. It means you need to make more communicative friends, and even better - a coach who will listen and inspire. Visit a psychologist for deep philosophical conversations, find new directions in life, hobbies and a circle of people who are interested in talking about it.

2. Time. You need a companion, a leisure partner. Most of all, you are afraid to stay alone for weekends and holidays, you often make some plans, but realizing that there is no one to share them with, you get upset and cancel everything. Once again, make friends, learn to plan your time and enjoy what is happening. Perhaps it just seems to you that you cannot have a pleasant dinner in your favorite restaurant alone with yourself, go to the cinema or go on vacation alone. Try it - what if you like it?

3. *Help*. You need real support because you are afraid of life's difficulties. Someone like you needs to be protected and your chosen one should become a "daddy" for you. You are waiting for a kind "elve" who will come and cope with all your problems at once. The way out of this situation is to make a list of things that you are afraid of and things that can give you a feeling of stability. Determine which of the indicated points you can decide on your own, and where you need support (just proceed from available, and not imaginary resources). Services like specialist "by the hour" will be your assistants.

4. *Gifts*. You need recognition and "sacrifices" in the form of gifts and deeds from your beloved man. This is how you understand love. This is a bit like the infantile position "Everyone owes me!", so think what exactly they "must give and present," and start pampering yourself. Give presents, arrange surprises and perform small or major feats for yourself.

5. *Touches*. Do you have a tactile hunger, and it seems that nobody embraced you with love for ages? In this case, the way out is sex and gentle touches. Take a lover without a lofty agenda and illusions. And try to surround yourself with items that are agreeable to the touch: cashmere or silk clothes, a teddy bear with whom you watch TV, soft slippers and a blanket, fluffy towels ... And more often pamper your body with a bath with aromatic foam, take a series of massage. At first glance, it seems that you need everything at once, but this is not so - some need definitely comes to the fore, so from it you should start the fight against loneliness.

MINUTE OF WISDOM
Don't try to please everyone.
Manage to please yourself.
M. Litvak

INFORMATION FOR REFLECTION
Basic love is love for yourself. It is the most important. And these are not so many feelings as actions.
M. Litvak

Coach exercise "My style of freedom"

Determine the prime cause using questions:

Why do you want to get rid of loneliness? What benefits will it bring to your life?

_____

_____

What exactly did you usually take offense at when you had relations?

_____

_____

What good things do you remember about past relationships?

_____

_____

How do you usually show love towards your partner, in what way?

_____

_____

How do you know that your partner loves you?

_____

_____

Different people - different loneliness. For some it is freedom, for others, it is a prison. But the choice, as always, is up to you. Fill this period of life with love for yourself, attention to others, devote your time to hobbies, instead of sadness and waiting for the miracle of eternal love. Start enjoying life. After all, as the Austrian psychologist, Viktor Frankl wrote more than half a century ago: "Happiness is like a butterfly. The more you try to catch it, the more it escapes. "

Be as active as possible in your search for love, but always remember that you can be happy regardless of the situation. **Treat yourself the way you would like your boyfriend to treat you!**

MINUTE OF WISDOM

If love is important for you, be that love.
Feel it and spread it around you.
If attention is important for you, be that attention.
Feel it and spread it around you.
If confidence is important for you, be that confidence.
Feel it and spread it around you.
And then you stop needing it - you create it!
Alunika Dobrovolskaya, Life-coach

Psychology of failures: why are you alone?

I will get you acquainted with three psychological theories that will explain the reasons for failure in your personal life. Do not be afraid of scientific formulations - I will try to explain them in an accessible way. Some things are desirable to understand and know if you are applying for the proud title of "intellectual person".

The formula for personal happiness is quite simple - it is when your capability, desire, and duties are equal. But why is it so difficult to be in agreement with yourself and balance these three concepts in your life?

The first reason is the so-called "ambivalence of desires" (conflict of goals).

This is the inability to make an unambiguous decision. Sigmund Freud believed that ambivalence is when two opposing motivations coexist inside you, that is, you strive simultaneously for two or more mutually exclusive situations. The chaos of impulses in our brains makes us want and not want something at the same time.

For example, you understand that in order to meet somebody you need to register on dating sites, make a bunch of dates, actively visit places where representatives of the opposite sex gather, to go somewhere, to communicate, to strengthen and expand your social ties, and you actually wish it. But at the same time, you want to stay at home with delicious ice cream and an interesting book or TV series. Your will (power) is, actually, directed forward and backward, left and right at the same time. Tension, psychological discomfort is created, but you still cannot decide …

And the more time it takes to hold conflicting impulses, the more a person gets worn out, the more difficult it is for him to choose a strong and independent personality. He spends a supply of psychic energy, which is needed in order to achieve goals, and this process deprives him of his will. It often leads to the fact that he is not able to choose one option, as a result, he refuses to decide at all or automatically chooses that method of action, that desire, which has more experience and which is simpler.

MINUTE OF WISDOM
Life is what happens to you when you're busy making other plans.
From a John Lennon song

The second reason is "cognitive dissonance" (internal conflict).
This is a state of mental discomfort, which is caused by a clash in a person's consciousness of conflicting ideas, beliefs, thoughts about something. This concept was introduced into psychology by Leon Festinger in 1957.

There are two systems inside us - excitement and inhibition, we strive for benefits and avoid losses, by the way, often imaginary, invented. These systems are supported by our inner philosophy - the sum of reflections, beliefs, life experiences.

For example, when we believe in true love, we think "Love is a life purpose!", and at the same time we know that falling in love can be painful, we had disappointments, we learn that "Love is a pain!" Then in the field of our consciousness, there are mutually exclusive concepts - and we doubt.

Doubt consumes vital force. And instead of trying, exploring new opportunities, integrating new experiences, a person, in order to reduce discomfort, tries to bypass situations in which discomfort can increase, that is, avoids communication, new meetings, and dates.

The most deplorable sight is caused by a person who cannot unequivocally form an opinion about himself - he constantly doubts himself, now "goddess/ hero", now "nonentity." There is no time for efficiency, all of a person's energy is consumed by an internal struggle.

INFORMATION FOR REFLECTION
According to a study by psychologists from Michigan, Facebook helps people reduce their feeling of loneliness, but it does not make them happier.

The third reason is "incongruence" (inconsistency of parts of the system).

The term congruence was introduced by Carl Rogers. Congruence is integrity and sincerity when all parts of the personality work together solving an urgent life task. In this case, the person says that he thinks and feels, does what he wants. There is no inconsistency and opposition between his desires, thoughts and behavior. It is easy and pleasant to communicate with him.

Thus, incongruence is the absence of truth in a person when behavior is contrary to his own goals.

Why does it happen so?

All three reasons for failure and loneliness lie in people's incertitude, their subconscious fear of making a mistake and failing, in unconscious indulgence in their "secondary benefits", in emotional and intellectual immaturity. People, trying to justify themselves, to please, more and more often lie to themselves and others, as a result, they plunge into a maelstrom of illusory hopes, misunderstandings and delusions. This is how the "loser" within us wins.

Thanks to the plasticity of the brain, we can change ourselves and, as a result, our destiny, but we often prefer to stay in a conditioned comfort zone. Lack of self-confidence, of confidence in the stability of relationships, fear of loss and of the unknown - all this turns on the emergency brake. No circumstances can stop a person on the way to his goals more than himself.

The tension inside a person is always transmitted to the outside and, basically, nobody wants to be close to such a person, to get acquainted, and to communicate.

SMILE

18-year-old Katya, who has been fond of psychology since the fifth grade, dreamed not of a prince, but of an idiot. And, having got married, unlike her friends, she did not receive moral and psychological trauma.

What to do?

You don't need to strive to become perfect, because no one is perfect, and it is important to remember that uncertainty and doubt are a part of our life. You cannot control the world, other people, but you are able to control your thoughts, desires, your life, that's why:

- recognize the reality, whatever it is and understand what you need;
- learn to make decisions and focus on them;
- be behaviorally flexible.

The world is a large reservoir of possibilities, it is abundant. It is important to send the right messages to it: your **thoughts, intentions, actions**.

A person who does not achieve what he wants starts to get sick with it, if he does not reconsider his experience in time and does not understand how to do it differently. Yes, it happens that it is already difficult for a person himself to untie a tangled skein of inconsistencies, and an outside view is needed to figure out who he is and where the exit is. You can always consult the experts, try to see how effective a new approach will be in your case. **Acquire the ability to see the cause-and-effect relationships in your life, to understand the essence of what is happening, to adequately respond to your own and other people's behavior, to change ideas about the world and about yourself based on new facts, and to notice new opportunities.**

Kill hope first! Sure, it's okay to hope for the best, but it's not okay to live and make decisions basing on hope. It is better to live by faith and in anticipation and expectation of the best: after all, you have done everything possible for this. You need to get in touch with reality. No, not to reconcile it, but to understand how to reconcile your desires and duties so that it would be easy to solve life's problems. Easy does not mean most simply, or quickly or effortlessly. "Easy" means the best way for yourself, and so that it makes you stronger and freer in the end.

Hope is a groundless thought that everything will be as you want, it "gives" you a feeling of helplessness, you try not to notice real obstacles. It's easier, but in the end, an aim to suppress a deeply embedded negativity appears, and this illusion can deprive you of the feeling of control over your life and peace of mind. Only decisiveness will help you to get out of this swamp. It is easy to check whether you finally took the decision seriously or not: **if the decision was made, then actions followed. If there are no actions, then there was no decision.**

MINUTE OF WISDOM
"And God stepped out on space,
And he looked around and said:
I'm lonely —

I'll make me a world"
J. W. Johnson, American writer, poet, publicist

INFORMATION FOR REFLECTION
Bert Hellinger's Ten Superphrases

1. Success has a mother's face.

2. In the eyes of our partner we look for our mother's eyes, disregarding whether we are male or female.

3. Those, who have a large stomach, carry their mother inside it. Mother, I reject you and thus carry you in my stomach.
(If you have a big stomach, whether you are a man or a woman, you have complaints about your mother. Do you want to lose weight? Get rid of those complaints!)

4. Father's daughter does not respect men.
(A daughter who adores her father idealizes his qualities. Then all other men seem worthless compared to him.)

5. Anger is a disappointment. Anger on your wife is disappointment in your mother.

6. Jealousy is an action towards parting with the partner.

7. Guilt and shame lead to death.

8. Those who drink alcoholic beverages want to die.

9. The unfair things I do to other people become my own fate.

10. To suffer is a lot easier than change. In order to become happy, one needs to have courage.

LESSON 4

CHANGE YOURSELF!

IF YOU WANT TO CHANGE THE SITUATION, CHANGE YOUR BEHAVIOR IN IT. IF YOU WANT TO CHANGE A PERSON, CHANGE YOURSELF.

A man is essentially a researcher - he likes to perceive the unknown, to expand into new territories. So set him a problem: how he can conquer and make this gorgeous, fascinating, incomprehensible and beautiful woman fall in love with him. It's about you!

You shouldn't think about him constantly, fantasize about how your love relationship can develop, savor the details with your friends. No, change your tactics! The task is to make him constantly think about you, guess, want to please, evoke a feeling of love. Let him bother his head over who you are, make assumptions and guesses. The more he thinks about you, the better.

Actually, the process of the emergence of love in a person is a constant concentration of thoughts on an object. After all, as soon as you become predictable for a man, he will get bored, there will be nothing more to explore. And he will disappear, striving for new horizons and heights. At the same time, give him hope and show attention, praise in order to make his sports interest constantly warm up.

And if you want to see a REAL man next to you, then there is only one way out - to become a REAL woman!

If you want to change the attitude (behavior) of a man towards you, then influence the deep layers of his psyche, that is, his beliefs and values. To penetrate into the soul of a person, to make him fall in love with you, you definitely need to know by what rules he lives. Who does he think he is? What is important, valuable in his life? This information is the key to his heart. To possess it, listen closely to him and conclude, make notes. What does he talk about (exactly "talk about", not "say"), where does he include emotions? And let him understand that next to you he will be able to receive from his life what is important for him, that with you he can become who he considers himself to be or who he wants to become.

And remember, only people with complementary or similar values have the happiest relationships.

MINUTE OF WISDOM

A child is always able to teach an adult three lessons: he is cheerful for no reason, always busy with something and knows how to achieve what he wants at all costs.

Mark Twain

New habits - new you!

Becoming a love magnet is a very tempting prospect and a worthy goal.

There is no better incentive for personal growth than a loved one next to you, for whose sake you want to become better. But even if he is not next to you yet, to begin with, become such a person for yourself.

Everything is allowed! Interdicts do not work, they only increase stress and weaken the will. Do not forbid yourself, but remind why you need it. Try to negotiate with yourself.

Discipline is more important than motivation. Jim Rohn said: "Motivation is what gets you started. Habit is what keeps you going. " Indeed, motivation can weaken or leave you for a while, and habits will stay with you forever. It makes sense to transform the necessary activity into useful habits, that is, make it automatic.

Educate yourself. Analyze your harmful mental, psychical, behavioral habits, and try to replace them with useful ones.

Habits play a big role in making dreams come true. Albert Einstein said: "Insanity is doing the same thing over and over again and expecting different results." Besides, good habits improve character.

A habit is formed within 30–66 days. The more complex is the behavior we want to make habitual, the more time we need.

Imagine the consequences. A couple of minutes of thinking about how you will regret not going to the gym will help you find the strength to get off the couch and transfer to the exercise machine.

Do not scold yourself for mistakes and laziness. Treat yourself like your best friend and boldly forgive your weaknesses. By forgiving yourself, you prohibit your brain from tempting you into instant indulgences, procrastination, and abandoning the inevitable stress of change. A scientific explanation for this came from Stanford professor Kelly McGonigal. She found that guilt-laden brains are particularly susceptible to temptation. It happens because our brain protects not only the health of its owner but also his mood. And therefore, while you blame yourself for laziness and weakness, it tries to support you and sends you impulses like:

"Okay, mistress, don't be upset. Better please yourself - prescind! Eat a delicious cake! And here are cute cats on Facebook! "

Hold on for 10 minutes to strengthen your will. Do not deny yourself pleasure, but say "No!" to seduction for at least 10 minutes, postpone the action after the first impulse for a while, and perhaps you will be able to get carried away by another. Try to turn on the "Stop and Think!" mode. Breathing exercises will help: 2 min. breathe in and out slowly and think during this process.

Make all the important decisions in the morning. It is in the morning that your will is strongest.

Learn the "art of small steps" and be patient. If the task is above your strength and you are trying to evade its completion, make it very small. The main thing is to start and not stop the process, gradually you will feel that you can do more.

Remember that great success consists of small daily victories. Gradually introduce new habits, stimulate and encourage new behaviors.

Real-life changes always take place at the action level. New actions create new behavioral habits, and new habits create a new destiny. "The only difference between winners and losers is that the winners act!" Anthony Robbins said. Ask yourself the question constantly: "Do I choose what is better for me or what is easier?".

Better doesn't always mean effortless, or fast, or simple, but it makes you stronger and happier in the end.

Start and don't stop. Even if you don't really want to do something, start doing it, it can carry away, and you won't be able to stop. Real change is impossible without effort.

Use an "if-then" planning strategy in order to slough off bad habits or instill new ones. "If" - Describe the triggers, situations that provoke unwanted behavior. Detail the situations and your desired reaction. Create causal relationships in your brain. In such a way it will be easier to stick to the plan and train your will, but not to thin it. The more you use the potential of your willpower, the more you spend it.

Learn to negotiate with yourself. Ask yourself a question before any decision: "How much from 1 to 10 do I NEED it? How much from 1 to 10 do I WANT it?" Before any action, ask yourself the question: "Is it EASIER for me or BETTER?" Choose the best one that leads you to happiness and success. Find a balance between these concepts. There is no need to "break" yourself, learn to negotiate with yourself. The method and ways of implementing your decisions in life should suit you and be acceptable, for pleasure, so that the temptations of self-sabotage and laziness do not arise. That is, the actions should bring pleasure in the process and satisfaction as a result.

Celebrate the completion of any action. After doing something, ask yourself the question: "Have I do what I wanted?" If the answer is "Yes!" - put yourself a tick "Achieved!"

Don't strive for perfection. Don't try to do everything and live perfectly. Trust me, "Enough" is better than "Excellent."

SMILE

- I love you!
- You are great.
- And you?
- And I'm great too.

Coach exercise "Personal happiness in 7 days"

Imagine that you have only 7 days to arrange your personal life. What will you do?

What will be your first steps?

Where will you go first of all, armed with a charming smile, enthusiasm, confidence in your heart?

How to be a Muse?

Lately, I often think about what it means to be a woman. How to learn to be socially successful in our demanding modern world and at the same time remain a seductive, attractive woman? How not to lose the elusive feeling of your fragility in this world, so that the men around you retain the desire to be "knights in shining armor"? How to learn to steer a middle course, so as not to turn from successful into courageous, and from attractive - into a silly coquette? The task is difficult. But doable.

To begin with, let's define the tasks that nature and history set for a woman. The main task of any woman is the ability to elevate her man, inspire him to heroism and thereby help civilization to develop. Being a muse is the fundamental privilege of women in history and in nature. It is not for nothing that a great woman has always been behind the success of every outstanding man. To inspire means to believe in a person. After all, if a worthy in all respects, real women is next to a man, then he will want to straighten up and correspond.

In my consultations, I often hear from men that they want to be loved, understood and inspired by their women. And if we know how to love, we try to understand, then to inspire ... A rare woman can clearly explain how to do it. Let's learn it!

We cannot force a man to be better. Trying to remake an adult man for yourself is lost labor! But we can do a lot to make him WANT to become better. For the sake of love!

Let's start with the basics. Go to the mirror and honestly ask yourself the question: Would you like to be better for the sake of the one you see in the mirror?

Is the answer "No"? Save the situation urgently! From now on, start turning into a muse, both externally and internally.

Appearance is evaluated first, a man loves with his eyes - this is commonplace. But commonplace, as we know, is a truth confirmed a thousand times! Lipstick, stockings, beautiful underwear, manicure, dress - this is the alphabet of femininity, do not forget about it.

Let's go deeper: in order to inspire someone, you need to have an inner core, to be a person whose opinion is esteemed, to feel your value and uniqueness. What makes you different from thousands of other women? What good things about you and your life can you share with your loved one? Actually, why should he be with you? Assess your potential clearly. Improve yourself to be proud of yourself and respect yourself. Respect is a conscious and indispensable condition for real, not ostentatious, self-love. Only if you feel harmony within yourself, know how to communicate with yourself, support yourself properly, to accept your disadvantages, to be proud of the positive that you have in you, you will be able to evaluate another person adequately, to see the good in him and stimulate his personal growth.

Before influencing other people, you need to learn how to influence yourself and be able to inspire yourself to improve.

Now let's imagine that you are outwardly flawless and inwardly ready to inspire. What's next?

And next, we'll talk about behavior. What exactly should you do, how to behave in order to inspire and elevate? Remember: a person is driven by profit. **It should be beneficial for your man to make his and your life better.** Encourage his every slightest achievement, develop and appreciate his best qualities. Start behaving with him as if he already meets all your requirements. Admire out loud, especially in front of others, consult with him, stroke his shoulders (it removes aggression). Learn to trust your man, do not teach him to live, better help him with admiration. Wide eyes, a pleased, happy smile, a delicious dinner - this will flatter him and will serve you well. **Be an angel (from time to time) - and he will believe that life with you is Paradise.**

And in order not to lose this idyll and not to lose your support and belief in him, your admiration for him, he will be ready for many things. He will strive to become better! For you!

The main secret of relationship management is that if we want to change the other person, we must change ourselves and choose the behavior that brings us closer to our goals!

To make a demigod man out of an ordinary man, you must become yourself a goddess, a muse of his success. And then you will live on Olympus.

The art of the "female mystery"

Everyone says: men love mysterious women. And this is true, especially at the stage of flirting. Just sometimes we get stuck in one image for a long time, we stop changing, trying to please and not to ruin anything in the relationship. We are afraid to take risks, because of this we become boring and lose our attractiveness.

To be a mystery means to be interesting, unpredictable, intriguing, to be ambivalent. It is the ambiguousness in the image of Mona Lisa that makes her so mysterious and desirable. She is both restrained and seductive, and it is mesmerizing …

Being a true woman is an art, and its mastery lies in the ability to surprise with your versatility, but at the same time to be yourself. In other words, feel inner harmony in any state. It is important to learn to enter into different emotional states that are more beneficial for the present moment.

In relationships, we mainly use three emotional states, three tactics of behavior. Know how to use them according to the circumstances, change to make it interesting being with you.

To be a woman means to be different!
The emotional state of the "cheerful girl" should be most effectively demonstrated during flirting.

When to apply?
When you want to admire a man.
When you want to ask for something.

When you want to be taken care of and protected.
When you want to express your true feelings in plus or minus.
When you express gratitude, accept gifts and care.
When you need help.
When you need to believe in yourself and be brave.
When you want to whimper in order to make somebody feel sorry for you.
When you want to have fun.

What for?
To receive gifts and care.
To act sometimes on instinct.
To love yourself unconditionally.
To be light and to take flirting like a game.
Just because.

The child does not think about the impression he makes and the consequences, so people trust children. They touch. We want to teach children and put our soul into them, to protect and take care of them.

The emotional state "seducing goddess" is most effectively demonstrated during seduction.

When to apply?
When you need to inspire to actions.
When you need to charm and become attractive.
When you want to make a holiday for him.
When you need to fill him with energy.
When you need to fill all the space around with yourself.
When you need to believe in someone.
When you let a man go to exploits.
When it is necessary to get rid of fears: to be alone, not to be liked, etc.
When you have to distribute responsibilities and rights.
When you should demand justice.
When you need to forgive.
When you must say "No!"

What for?
To make a man feel like a hero.
So that he strives to be with you more often.
To feel confident.

To make a man proud of you.
To make him jealous, not you.
To be patient with the weaknesses of others.
For others to seek to capture your attention.
To feel worthy of the best in this life.

People are proud of a goddess, they respect her, they bow before her, they fear losing her favor and value her, they consult with her. They want to admire a goddess, for her sake a man is ready to conquer the world and throw it at her feet. She beckons, captivates with beauty and affection, her talents intoxicate. You forget about everything next to her! ..

The emotional state "careful mommy" is the most effective "demo version" of family life.

When to apply?
When you need to take care of your internal and external order.
When you need to take care of others.
When it is necessary to fill the space around with comfort.
When you want to support others and yourself.
When you need to defend your principles.
When it's necessary to scold someone.
When you need to husband resources (money, time, relationships) properly.
When you need to make household chores enjoyable.
When you need to get a job done.
When you need to understand and accept a man as he is.
What for?
To create an atmosphere of unconditional love around you.
To form home traditions.
So that others could feel carefulness, loyalty, protection in you.
To make a man feel at home like in a five-star all-inclusive hotel.

Only at our mommy's side we can switch off, stop fighting for a place in the sun, relax the mind. We want to tell her about everything because our mother will understand and will not judge. We want to cuddle up to her and feel like in childhood - calm and comfortable.

There is also the state of the "warrioress" - the modern Amazon of the concrete jungle, a woman who knows what she wants and firmly gets her way. But you should leave this state at work and do not bring it into your romantic life.

Now you are probably waiting for specific recommendations on how to bring this information to life? They will not be here! Make an effort and get creative - think about your own approach and style for each state, relying on your strengths and experience. The main thing is that you feel natural and comfortable in it. **Being a real woman means forgetting about templates. Down with predictability, be different - be yourself!**

Coach exercise "Getting into a role in 1 minute"

There are two reliable ways to correctly get into any desired psychological state.

1. You must remember the situation when you felt such as you want to appear now. Close your eyes, mentally rewind the tape, remember your feelings, and transfer them to the current moment.

2. You must imagine yourself as an animal, which, in your opinion, has the qualities you need. Feel like a panther or a kitten. You can mentally change the size of this animal: let it be either the size of a two-story house - for reinforcement, or a tiny fluffy ball curled up on your beloved's lap.

Become a gift for your man!

So, you are grimly determined to activate your personal life. You open the wardrobe and ... Oh, horrors! The eternal female problem: absolutely nothing to wear! Rather, there are a lot of clothes, but there is nothing to wear. A familiar state? And why? Because, judging by your wardrobe, you were not preparing to become a happy woman. Yes, you have prepared to be an office worker, a businesswoman, an aspiring athlete, an ambisexual, but not a bride, tender and fragile.

But, indeed, the contents of some women's wardrobes can be easily confused with the wardrobe of a low-performing teenage student: T-shirts, jeans and no romance. Unless only a pair of incomprehensible wonderbras, in which it is already inconvenient to undress in a "decent society". Let's start with them. The first thing that awakens a woman in you, and fantasies in the surrounding men, is underwear. Self-esteem rises sharply when you know that the underwear is on top. Even if no one sees it yet, this is your little secret. Here, in fact, you have become a little more mysterious. The lingerie should be flawless and shape-flattering.

The next stage is the dresses. The wardrobe of a "marriageable girl" should mainly consist of them: at least four dresses in winter and summer versions. In addition to the little black legend dress, choose wrap and shirt dresses as well - this is a classic and therefore a profitable investment. As for red dresses, Lady in Red should know that beige shoes are the best for such attire. And by the way, the sexiest color is beige, a flesh color, and not red, as is commonly believed, a beige color creates the illusion of no clothes. Forget about models with a small flower, a la grandma's dressing gown - they will not add any romance to your image.

Now about the footwear. You need black and beige shoes with nice heels. And do not try to increase your small growth through the height of the heel - it looks disproportionate. "Thumbelina" should try to choose models no higher than eight centimeters. Shoes and tights color must match - it will visually increase the length of the legs. I advise you to avoid platforms. They always seem like a hoof.

Try to invest in clothes, not spend money on them. Better put the thing in the store, come home, calm down and estimate if it is really necessary, if you have anything to wear it with, and if you really can not live without it. Maybe it's a matter of life and death, then go back and buy. If not, call the store, say to them that you changed your mind, and apologize politely.

When a leopard thing suddenly appears in your wardrobe, and this is how many girls try to stand out and evoke the hunting instinct of the opposite sex, remember the rule of wearing such an element of the wardrobe - it must be expensive (this also applies to lace works and clothes with rhinestones) and no more than one thing per look. Shoes, or a dress, or a blouse. And it's better if the rest of the style is restrained: a pencil skirt, hair tied in a ponytail, glasses in a strict frame. Then it looks spicy and tasteful. Translucent blouses look pretty tempting. Just do not forget to put on a tight tank top under them - only the hands and the cleavage should be visible. Here it will be appropriate to recall the mini-wardrobe options. First, decide what you want to show the world: legs or cleavage - but only one thing, not all at once. Know how to distinguish the style of the seductress from vulgarity or excessive eroticism. After all, your primary goal is to charm a man, and not to get him into bed.

A white shirt is multifunctional, it does not require special financial costs and looks sexy. It seems as if you have stolen it from your boyfriend's or older brother's wardrobe. It is better if it is starched, vibrant and sharply white.

Creole earrings are sexy. Thin large rings are beautiful and inexpensive, and loose well-coiffed hair will complement the image of a fatal beauty. Do not forget to ask your loved one about his idea of beauty. What clothes look feminine to him?

It is interesting that, according to the results of psychological researches, it has emerged that women try to dress sexually not so much for men as for their own kind. Yes! We strive to look sexy for women, thereby, actually demonstrating ourselves and signaling that the rival must get out of the way. So it's better to go shopping with a professional shopping consultant than with a friend.

Clothes worth spending money on
Coat
Fluffy tricot
Blouses
Fur
Evening dress

INFORMATION FOR REFLECTION
Many years ago I read The Code of a Really True Woman on the pages of a glossy magazine. I cut it out so that I never forget the basics of femininity, and today I want to share this information with you.

The Code of a Really True Woman
A True Woman loves to rub creams into her skin, and a Really True Woman buys those creams that are absorbed by themselves.

On a True Woman, attires look amazing, and a Really True Woman looks amazing in such attires.

A True Woman pedicures in the summer, and a Really True Woman does it regardless of the season.

A True woman hides that she is smart. A Really True Woman is not going to hide it.

A True Woman will refuse the dessert, and a Really True Woman will eat it, and then she will starve for a week. But she will never admit that she is on a diet.

A True Woman appreciates a pleasant male company. And a Really True Woman is appreciated by this company.

A True Woman wins her rivals, and a Really True Woman does not have them.

A True Woman is a gift for her husband. A Really True Woman selects a husband as a gift for her.

A True Woman will not show that she is bored in the company. A Really True Woman will leave the company a minute before she gets bored.

A True Woman dresses up to please others. A Really True Woman - to please herself.

A True Woman is secretly jealous. And a Really True Woman at the first reason for jealousy forgets about the existence of this man.

A True Woman ruins herself if she likes a thing, and a Really True Woman finds someone to ruin.

A True Woman follows the advice of fashion magazines. A Really True Woman is a source of inspiration for them.

Wardrobe items to save on

Fortunately, savings can be made when arranging a wardrobe. We are not talking about poor quality things, but about those things that are inexpensive.

Jeans
Trousers
Skirts
Classic shirt with buttons
Light jersey
T-shirts and A-shirts

Change your usual thinking style!

It seems to all of us that as soon as a Prince Charming appears at the threshold of our hearts, the door will open ... And a continuous feast of Love and mutual understanding will begin. We, like Sleeping

Beauties, all hope for the magic kiss from the one that will color our gray everyday life with a palette of emotions.

Stop waiting for Great Love - live and enjoy your life here and now.

Nobody will fill your life with joy and meaning if you are not able to do it yourself. It is impossible to transform from a sad person into a joyful and cheerful person immediately. Therefore, get ready for the fateful meeting with the Man of your Dreams in advance - enjoy your life!

We often blame the situation and people that our feelings have died out and have not brought Love and the expected Happiness into our lives. But in fact, it is we, or rather our little thoughts, to which we do not attach great importance, destroy all wonderful undertakings. And the more often we say a phrase inside, and the more passion we demonstrate (the emotional background is the energy of thought, which is its power), the higher the likelihood that it will become a self-fulfilling prophecy. And it is in our power to monitor thought viruses and replace them with useful paradigms.

SMILE
Every time I look at a cream cake, I imagine myself in a beautiful, body-hugging, short dress and think: WHY DO I NEED THIS DRESS?

INFORMATION FOR REFLECTION
Coaching is based on Milton Erickson's five principles. These principles help to overcome your limitations and achieve your desired goals.
1. *All people are okay.*
2. *Each person already has all the necessary resources.*
3. *Each person always makes the best choice.*
4. *A person's intentions are always positive.*
5. *Change is inevitable.*

Harmful thoughts are different, here are the most common.

1. I have no time.

It may mean that you are afraid of new disappointments or are not interested in these relationships (they do not have the realization of your values).

2. I will meet my Love.

There is a difference between the partner we need and the one we dream of. Dreams are often illusions that we waste time and energy on, and at this point we abandon relationships that could bring comfort and peace of mind.

3. I'm not good enough.

People fall in love not only with ideal ones. Rather the opposite - small weaknesses make people more attractive. Besides, no one forbids you to improve yourself for love.

4. It's too complicated.

As long as you think so, it happens. The comfort of being alone is a swamp. It's warm, of course, but weighs down.

5. If he ... If I ... (there is a place for all sorts of fantasies)

It happened as it happened. Self-torture has never strengthened relationships.

6. I am unlucky in love.

The real failure is to come to terms with the existing situation and stop trying. Sometimes it's better to pause, but not give up on the dream.

7. He must ...

Nobody must love you. They either want to love you or not. And there are many reasons for that, many of which you are not able to influence.

8. Everything is great with us (when it is not so).

When it seems to you that something is wrong in your relationship, then it does not seem to you. It's time to be honest about your feelings and find a solution.

9. They are all the same!

Experience can do a disservice. Give a person an opportunity and time to show his best qualities. Evaluate a man by his actions, but not through the prism of stereotypes.

10. My heart is broken!

I don't need new risks. Let the past go and believe in the best. It is possible that right now God has prepared a gift for you.

Coach Exercise "Belief Detox"

Review all thoughts, proverbs, sayings, beliefs that relate to you and the "Love" sphere. Everything that has accumulated over the years in the pantry "Personal life". Write them all on a sheet, cross out unnecessary ones. Leave the useful ones and make them permanent.

Complete sentences that will help you understand yourself and make a list of helpful beliefs. Each list should contain 5-6 items:

My happiness is hindered by...

_____

_____

In order to feel like a person 5% more worthy of happiness...

_____

_____

Love is...

_____

_____

Good men...

_____

_____

If I refuse to live by the values that other people have imposed on me...

_____

_____

If I succeed in love...

_____

_____

If I allow myself to be loved ...

_____

_____

When I learn to appreciate myself...

_____

_____

To make my life 5% happier ...

_____

_____

In order to meet the man of my dreams ...

_____

_____

I begin to understand that ...

_____

_____

To love means ...

_____

_____

If I want to become the woman of his dreams, I need ...

_____

_____

If I want love to come into my life, I need ...

_____

_____

I realize more and more clearly ...

_____

_____

If I take on more responsibility for fulfilment of my desires ...

_____

_____

If I let go of the reins and allow myself to experience what love is ...

_____

_____

LESSON 5

BE CHEERFUL!

OF ALL WOMEN, MEN CHOOSE THE MOST CHEERFUL. OF THE CHEERFUL - THE MOST BEAUTIFUL. OF THE BEAUTIFUL - THE WISEST.

All living beings in nature strain towards the light. And we are as radiant as our thoughts are. Happiness makes people more sociable, more responsive, happy people are liked by themselves and others more, they manage conflicts better, their immune system works better.

Behave like a happy person in order to feel happier: try walking with a more relaxed, springy gait, straightening your shoulders, waving your hands lightly, gesturing a little more expressively, using positive emotional words such as "like", "adore", "love".

Think with a plus sign. It is impossible to be a radiant personality if you don't have effulgent thoughts. Radiant thoughts will attract positive to your destiny! **Learn to see the joy in small things, to notice the good in yourself, in others, in the world.** Thanks to cognitive distortions, it is easier for our brain to notice the bad, it does this on autopilot, but the joy must be noticed consciously. And this is a special wisdom that only happy people possess.

Try to analyze your usual thoughts and cleanse your inner space of those thought viruses that prevent you from achieving success. You can do it with a simple exercise: set yourself a reminder for every half hour and write down what you think at that moment. Analyze - delete unnecessary thoughts.

Give thanks - gratitude returns energy. Think about the amazing things in your life, about all the people you love, about everything that is dear to your heart. Every day, mark 3-5 the most important values in your life, for which you are especially grateful to fate at the moment, vividly experiencing a feeling of gratitude and admiration. For example, thank the Universe for the beautiful world around, parents - for love, higher powers - for good luck, friends - for support, loved ones - for attention, ill-wishers - for an incentive to growth and development, etc. The psychological fact is that grateful people feel happier and more energetic.

INFORMATION FOR REFLECTION

Jenny Levine (book "Harper's Bazaar. Great Style") believes that while the expensive purchase can be difficult, there are some things that are really worth spending money on. They will be worn so often that in the end they will justify the money spent on them.

Share your love. Think about what you love, about the people you love, and send everyone a ray of your love. You feel joy and warmth when, even in your thoughts, you give others love. **Family and close friends are the most important source of a happy life.**

Attract good luck. Noticing any, even the smallest, luck, you become luckier and luckier every day, and such people are always interesting and attractive. By focusing your attention on luck, positivity and gratitude, you magically become an optimistic and cheerful, attractive woman.

Develop your emotional intelligence. A woman capable to inspire and to make fall in love is always in harmony with her feelings and thoughts. Put your inner world in order! Train your inner honesty. Do not try to avoid negative emotions, because everything in this world has its own meaning. Repressed emotions do not go anywhere, but only accumulate and destroy us from within, deprive us of energy and a sense of the taste of life. Pessimistic, peremptory internal comments (automatic thoughts) undermine self-confidence and depression, trigger negative emotions, and increase anxiety, fatigue, and stress in your life.

Develop your virtue. The ancient Greeks noted four virtues: prudence, fortitude, justice, temperance. Socrates considered intelligence to be the source of virtue and called prudence the highest virtue, which unites all the others.

We like kind people. Ask questions: "What kind deed do I want to do today?", "What kind deed have I done today?", "To whom do I want to give my sincere attention, kind word, support?" Good deeds give a feeling of happiness, improve character and relationships with others, transform the world around you, and attract good luck into your destiny. People like to return the favor, and the better we are to a person, the more we like him.

Negative emotions serve negative beliefs, and emotions manage your life energy. It's up to you to choose which feelings to set in motion. Of course, you cannot control the first reaction to the situation, but you are responsible for your conclusions and actions.

Say about others good things or nothing. If you say positive and pleasant things about friends and colleagues, then you will also be considered a pleasant person.

Notice the beauty and joy of every day. The feeling of happiness is 50% genetically programmed, 40% depends on your own behavior and only 10% on external circumstances. Always look for the good and the beautiful things around you, and you do not need to wait for special events or circumstances to enjoy your life. Ask yourself more often questions during the day: "What good do I notice in this situation, person, myself? What do I feel grateful for? What pleases me here and now?"

SMILE

It is harmful for women to watch movies about love, and for men - porn movies. Both, those and others begin to think that it is possible in real life.

Coach exercise "WOW effects"

Every day write down three of the most enjoyable WOW effects of the day. Look for something or someone to admire, something to enjoy, and write down every day at least three joys of the day. In the moments of joy and admiration, say to yourself with admiration: "Wow!", Feeling how a "lamp of happiness and love" is lit in your heart. A light, relaxed, happy smile will appear on your lips, and your eyes will sparkle. By keeping your attention on the positive moments of the day for 5, 10, 20 seconds longer than usual, note your positive emotions and sensations in the body.

Develop! Quotes, wise phrases, anecdotes, new foreign words, new knowledge and understandings... New useful information develops you, making you spiritually richer, deeper, more attractive.

Take time to strengthen your sense of humor daily: after dinner read an anecdote, a joke, watch a funny video. Laughter prolongs life!

INFORMATION FOR REFLECTION

Life wisdom

1. If you want to live in peace, do not confer any benefits when you are not asked about it. Otherwise, you will become a deliverer and fall into the triangle of fate (pursuer - deliverer - victim).

2. There are 3 components of life: changes, choice and principles.

3. Live proceeding from your imagination, not your story.

4. Feeling of guilt turns off the brain.

5. Life is 10% what happens to us, and 90% our reaction to it.

6. What the wise man does at the beginning, the fool does at the end.

7. Our life always benefits people. It serves as either an example or a warning to them.

8. The better our present, the less we think about the past.

9. Nobody lives twice, but many people do not know how to live even once.

10. Life is an ocean. It is difficult to swim on rough surfaces. Those who are weak go down to the bottom: it's quieter there.

11. Living a mile can be a punishment, and living an inch can be a blessing. You do not need to solve all life's problems at once, you need to solve only the problems of today. You are required to endure only the pain of this moment.

12. The wonderful expression "bel far niente" means "the joy of doing nothing."

13. Falling is a part of life, getting up is living it. Being alive is a gift, and being happy is your choice.

14. Personality is a signature on the water. You haven't signed up yet, and it has already gone.

15. For better or worse, never take life too seriously: you can't get out of it alive in any case.

16. In order to be fully connected with another person, you must first find a connection with yourself. If we cannot come to terms with our loneliness, we begin to use another person as a shelter from isolation.

17. A battle for life or life for the sake of battles - everything is in our hands.

18. If you put a hungry lion, a man, a chimpanzee, a baboon and a dog in a large cage, it is clear that the man will be eaten first!

19. Greed and happiness have never met each other. It is not surprising that they are not acquainted.

20. Life is poetry, not a commodity on the market. If you try to be helpful, you will be used. You will be restrained because the world cannot throw practical people away.

21. A person can laugh or cry. Whenever you cry, you could laugh - it's up to you to choose.

Enjoy your femininity!

If you ask a modern woman to explain to herself why a Man is needed, you will get a fairly stereotyped list, each item from which she is theoretically able to satisfy independently or without the need to enter into long-term relations.

A similar situation, exactly the opposite, will happen to a modern man. It turns out that on a conscious, social level, we do not need each other. A sad but important realization. But! We need each other on a deeper, biological level.

Men and women attract each other as "plus" and "minus", striving to bring to life the idea of nature: to complement and develop each other, to create common energy for the development and prosperity of civilization. But we do it badly because we implement the tasks of society, which often contradict the laws of nature. Ignorance of the laws, as they say, does not relieve us of responsibility, that is why so many smart and beautiful women are single (even being married!), deeply unhappy, dissatisfied, cynical and embittered.

Man's world

We live in a man's world, in conditions of fierce competition and relentless struggle for success. As Donald Trump said: "The biggest success comes when you swim against the tide." And so, overcoming all his desires, the winner is the one who lives according to the principle of duties.

Rigidity (to wipe out all rivals), firmness, ambition, assertiveness, determination, logical and analytical thinking help to survive and succeed in the jungle of modern life. Just like hundreds of thousands of years ago, people are fighting for prey, result, achievement, power. Although there is one distinguishing feature of our time - now the beautiful half of humanity is actively participating in this battle for resources. And I must admit, very successfully.

In direct progression to the number of successful businesswomen, an army of women dissatisfied with their life, who in the evenings, after working days, the dream of simple women's happiness, is growing.

An independent, self-sufficient, free modern woman can often outwardly leave in the dust any top model. For hours she "makes herself" in gyms, facial rooms and plastic surgery units, learns the tricks of NLP and comprehends the mysteries of intimate gymnastics.

Life is a struggle! A man is a trophy! Other women are competitors! Any means to an end! The main thing is not to relax! She also tries to use men's strategies in matters of relationships, because she does not know others.

Adult female qualities: affection, warmth, cheerfulness, gullibility, tenderness, tolerance, compassion, so attractive for real men, are not developed in her and remained at the level of childish infantile qualities. Therefore, she becomes completely unprotected and confused when it comes to relationships with her beloved man, experiencing childhood resentment or guilt instead of the desire and ability to give her own love, share her feminine energies, and take responsibility for her emotional state.

There is often a weak, resigned loser next to such a woman, whom she simply is not able to respect and admire really. A man with healthy male ambitions: successful, self-sufficient, realized, strong, responsible (and she wants to see him as her life partner) subconsciously fears such a woman and flees, following the natural instinct of self-preservation.

International scientific research does not add optimism: most women experience disruptions in the endocrine system and hormonal imbalances (an increase in the level of male sex hormones). Physiology dictates the psyche and vice versa.

What should the women who want to avoid loneliness and attract a worthy man with fulfilled ambitions, purposeful, successful, responsible, do?

A way out of this situation is possible: through the realization of your feminine task and role in nature!

INFORMATION FOR REFLECTION

There are two types of smiles. The first is a sincere, or Duchenne smile (after the name of its discoverer, neuropathologist Guillaume Duchenne). It can be recognized by the raised corners of the lips and crow's feet around the eyes. It is very difficult to consciously control the muscles that make you smile. Therefore, another type of smile - the so-called Pan-American (after the name of an unforgettable advertising clip of a famous airline that dazzled with the grin of the stewardesses) - looks unnatural and simulates more a grimace that appears on the face of a frightened monkey.

Looking at the photographs, an experienced psychologist at first glance can distinguish a Duchenne smile from a Pan-American smile. Taking advantage of this their "gift", specialists from Berkeley decided to conduct an interesting experiment. They studied 141 photographs of high school girls in school albums for 1960: except three girls, all people in the photos were smiling, and half of them had completely natural smiles. Then these, already adult women, were asked what their life was at the age of 27, 43 and 52 years. Conducting their survey in the 1990s, psychologists wanted to find out whether it is possible to predict a person's future from school photography. To their surprise, they found that schoolgirls who smiled naturally in photographs were, on average, more likely to get married, were married longer, and felt happier over the next 30 years.

Could it be that the "crow's feet" in the corners of the eyes served as a guarantee for this? Then scientists suggested: what if a sincerely smiling woman is simply more beautiful, and therefore their happy life is predetermined by external data, and not by the smile itself? They went back to albums, trying to appreciate the beauty of each girl. But it turned out that the appearance did not matter in this case. It's just that a sincerely smiling woman had more chances to successfully marry and be happy. The result of the study was a general conclusion: positive emotions fleetingly captured on film with a fair amount of probability.

Realize your female role!

Fortunately, the intellect of our contemporaries is developed excellently - so we will rely on the strengths of the weaker sex, we will try to get to the bottom of the truth with the help of logic.

The brain, like any governing body, strives for harmony, and it sees this harmony as the coherence of the perception of the world, oneself, and oneself in the world with the gained experience. Our women have more than enough experience, but the filters of reality perception require correction.

Our consciousness is a network of ideas that we successfully, or not successfully, implement through our actions, and the set of actions (our behavior) ultimately leads us to the corresponding results, a general feeling of life as a successful or unsuccessful fate.

Thus, we can perceive this world as a hostile environment that, for example, is a natural state for a man. According to a simple idea of nature, he is conceived as a bread-winner, who earns, makes money, fighting, contesting, "killing" and competing - this is how he realizes his male potential. And we can perceive the world as a "friendly environment" created for cooperation, prosperity, preservation and growth, developing and strengthening our natural feminine abilities and strategies that will ultimately lead to a more harmonious, and most importantly, happy female destiny.

No, it will not be a masculine way of instant results; it will take patience and faith. Feminine methods are smooth changes. You will correct your "world map" - the perception of the surrounding reality and yourself in this reality step by step. And then the perception of new yourself, new ideas and attitudes will help you live a happier, more fulfilling life and realize yourself in all areas of life that are important for a woman.

SMILE
An optimist and a pessimist meet.
Pessimist:
- Eh ... They have not invited me... Forgot...

Optimist:
- Wow! They have not invited me - REMEMBER!

Coach exercise "Smile"

Inure yourself to smile! Psychologists say that if you smile even for no reason and keep a smile on your face for 15-30 seconds, you will feel much happier. Put a reminder signal on your phone and smile every hour for 15 seconds.

TEST: "My femininity"

We all dream of a real man next to us. And let's think about what a real man dreams of, what kind of woman he wants to make his partner. The answer suggests itself: A Real Woman. It is logical ... and sad at the same time, because very few women, passing the test that I propose, generally understand what femininity is. Yes, in our time you need to have different qualities in order to achieve a goal. I agree one hundred percent, but nevertheless, we need to demonstrate the qualities that men expect from us in order to see us first of all as a woman, and only then as a pleasant companion and friend.

Fill in the table, in the first column, next to the definition of quality, put M, or F, or N (that is, this quality can be attributed to female, male or neutral (characteristic of both sexes) characteristics), and in the second column, determine on a scale from 1 to 10 to what extent this quality is inherent in you, and summarize at the end. This test is a list of 118 character traits, which was published by the American magazine Omni. The test allows us to check whether we correctly imagine what qualities men and women should be endowed with.

Characteristics	Male, female, neutral	To what extent this quality is inherent in me - from 1 to 10
1. Ability to amuse		
2. Ability to argue		
3. Ability to count on yourself		
4. Ability to empathize		
5. Ability to make a compromise		
6. Ability to make a person to change his opinion		
7. Ability to see a joke		
8. Ability to sympathise		
9. Ability to understand the acquaintance		
10. Ability to work		
11. Acerbity		
12. Acidity		
13. Activity		
14. Adulthood		
15. Advanced intuition		
16. Affectation		
17. Affection		
18. Aggressiveness		
19. Alertness		
20. Ambitiousness		
21. Analytical mind		
22. Animation		
23. Athleticism		
24. Attraction		
25. Brightness		
26. Carefulness		
27. Capacity for hegemony		
28. Cheerfulness		

29. Childishness		
30. Compassion		
31. Competitiveness		
32. Complexity of character		
33. Conservativism		
34. Contumacy		
35. Courage		
36. Culturalness		
37. Democratic character		
38. Diffidence		
39. Discipline		
40. Disorderliness		
41. Eccentricity		
42. Fashion following		
43. Femininity		
44. Fertile imagination		
45. Fidelity		
46. Force		
47. Fraility		
48. Frankness		
49. Gentilesse		
50. Gentleness		
51. Greed		
52. Gullibility		
53. Hard-working nature		
54. High moral character		
55. Honesty		
56. Hospitability		
57. Impetuousness		
58. Independence		
59. Indeterminism		
60. Individualism		
61. Intellect		
62. Irascibility		

63. Jealousy		
64. Jocundity		
65. Kindness		
66. Laziness		
67. Love for children		
68. Magnanimity		
69. Manner to speak in a low voice		
70. Meditativeness		
71. Mental speed		
72. Moderation		
73. Modesty		
74. Nonchalance		
75. Open-mindedness		
76. Optimism		
77. Own opinion		
78. Patience		
79. Perseverance		
80. Prettiness		
81. Proficiency		
82. Propensity for changes		
83. Propensity for domination		
84. Propensity for idealism		
85. Propensity for possession		
86. Propensity for power		
87. Propensity for risk		
88. Punctuality		
89. Purity		
90. Rejection of rudeness		
91. Reliability		
92. Respectfulness		
93. Ruse		
94. Self-assertion		
95. Self-assurance		

96. Self-belief		
97. Selfishness		
98. Sense of humor		
99. Sense of responsibility		
100. Sensibility		
101. Seriousness		
102. Sincerity		
103. Slackness		
104. Sociability		
105. Sophistication		
106. Solidness		
107. Tact		
108. Tenderness		
109. Tender-mindedness		
110. Tension		
111. Thaw		
112. Tolerance		
113. Unconcern		
114. Unusualness		
115. Vigorousness		
116. Virile character		
117. Vivacity		
118. Weakness for praise		

Male traits: 2, 3, 18, 20, 21, 23, 27, 31, 35, 46, 58, 60, 67, 77, 83, 86, 87, 94, 96, 116.

Female traits: 4, 5, 8, 9, 11, 17, 24, 26, 28, 29, 30, 38, 43, 45, 50, 52, 67, 69, 90, 108, 111, 118.

Neutral traits: 1, 6, 7, 10, 12, 13, 15, 14, 16, 19, 22, 25, 32, 33, 34, 36, 37, 39, 40, 41, 42, 44, 47, 48, 49, 51, 53, 54, 55, 56, 57, 59, 61, 62, 63, 64, 65, 66, 68, 70, 72, 73, 74, 75, 76, 78, 79, 80, 81, 82, 84, 85, 88, 89, 91, 92, 93, 95, 97, 98, 99, 100, 101, 102, 103, 104, 105, 106, 107, 109, 110, 112, 113, 115, 117.

If your choice does not differ much from the data in the table, and feminine qualities are inherent in you, you understand where, how and why you need to demonstrate them - it means that you have generally correct ideas of what men and women should be, and you have learned the lessons of this book well. If not, there is something to think about and something to strive for.

MINUTE OF WISDOM

Personally, I am very fond of strawberries and cream, but for some strange reason, fish prefers worms. That is why when I go fishing, I do not think about what I like, but what the fish likes.

Dale Carnegie

Myths about female weakness

In the modern world, it is difficult for a woman to be weak and successful at the same time. Society has a twofold attitude towards strong and intelligent representatives of the weaker sex and this attitude is often surrounded by myths. Here are some of them.

Myth 1. Men like weak women

In fact, they like strong and self-confident women. Because power itself is sexual, and multiplied by femininity and beauty, it becomes an impeccable weapon of seduction. A worthy man is capable of falling in love only with a woman whom he can respect and at the same time feel at ease with her. And this can only be realized with a self-confident, internally calm woman contented with herself and her life. It is necessary to demonstrate not material independence, but to show emotional and psychological resilience, the ability to behave slightly haughtily, from the height of one's wisdom and self-respect. Women's success is, first of all, success in relationships. Male success is an achievement in the material world.

Men do not like the metamorphoses that happen to beautiful ladies when they fall in love. Beautiful, self-sufficient women suddenly turn into squeezed, anxious, ingratiating fools in love, forgetting that they fell in love with them as independent and successful women for their uniqueness and strength of character. And it is so because there is an opinion in society: a man can like only forgivingly kind, tenderly sweet, compliant and slightly stupid woman. In the hope of making a love nest with a suitable male and because of fear to lose a promising relationship, women begin to simulate, not remembering that the one who overplays loses in the relationship.

Of course, the role of a "romantic child" also sometimes needs to be used, especially during flirting or when you want to ask for something, fool about for a while, cause him affection, the instinct of a defender, and give him a sense of security, your reliability. But at the same time, you need to remain yourself: estimable, with an inner core, with your own principles, plans and high self-esteem. The main thing is to remember: *men like not weak women, but those who know how to seem to be weak.*

Myth 2. Strong women need weak men

It is believed that self-sufficient and successful women should choose weaker men or gigolos as partners in order to avoid the struggle for power in relationships. Probably, each of us should make her own choice, but still, any woman, no matter how courageous she may seem to others, wants a reliable shoulder next to her and a partner whom you sincerely admire. Therefore, there is no point lowering the bar, but it will not hurt to learn behavioral agility. It is important to understand that at home, iron ladies should turn into domestic cats. When dealing with men, change your intellectual habits for wisdom, all-knowingness for intuition, and put on a soft glove of flattery and tenderness on a hard fist. Using your wits and charisma, learn to be a 3 in 1 woman - a mother, a friend, and a hetaera. Such are the women that strong men like - different. And only smart women are able to combine the uncombinable.

Also, remember that a **woman's initiative kills a relationship**, namely, its presence distinguishes the strong from the less self-confident, so pass it on to the man. Let him get the feeling that he is the leader, that he is the main one. A wise woman will be able to hint her beloved to the solution she needs. For example, suppose today you want to go to an Italian restaurant that has opened near your home. You can say: "Honey, I really want pizza ... By the way, have you seen an Italian restaurant opened? A neighbor said that there is excellent cuisine!" Supposed reaction: "Let's go there!" And you: "What an amazing idea!

With pleasure, dear! " And often caress the male ear with the phrase "As you say, dear!" After it, you can do as you see fit.

Go back from the desire to prove something, persuade and justify yourself. Forget about ultimatums, threats, assaults and any manifestation of aggressiveness - these are all signs of male behavior. Resentment, tears, sadness, ignorance are much more effective in dealing with men. Let yourself sometimes be capricious, especially when you are sick, ask his advice, ask for help and favors. Let your small feminine weaknesses waken in him a protector, mentor and rescuer - a strong man. A smart woman can always allow herself to play dumb. But just play, not be her.

SMILE

A crow has decided to fly to southern skies together with migratory geese.
Geese say:
- Crow, you won't reach the southern skies, you are not a migratory bird, our organism is different and anyway...
Crow:
- No! I am strong, I am cool, I will be able to do it.
Geese:
- Well, let's fly!
They fly a day, two days, a week. The flock arrives in the southern skies. The crow is hopelessly behind. The geese have been looking at the sky for a long time - they have not seen it. And then they have given a look and seen a dot in the sky. The crow with its last bit of strength, barely flapping its wings, lathery flies, falls next to the leader.
Geese:
- Well, crow, good job! You are so strong, so cool!
The crow, barely raising its head:
- Yes, I'm strong, I'm cool, but silly baggage! ..

MINUTE OF WISDOM
I will not say that it was a lucky break. I just deserve it.
Sharon Stone

We ourselves became those guys whom we wanted to marry in our youth.
Faina Ranevskaya

Myth 3. Men like silly women

From time to time pretending to be silly is one thing, but constantly being a fool is not to everyone's taste. And of course, we can find such people: full of complexes and dim-witted people like to seem educated and smart against the background of such girls. But a self-respecting man chooses a partner according to other parameters. He will be happy if there is one next to whom you can talk about everything in the world, receive wise female advice and support from her, and not an infantile cutesy doll. However, intelligence does not exclude beauty, and beauty does not exclude cared-for look. No matter how intellectual a woman is, there is no point to refuse with aversion cosmetics and beautiful outfits designed to exacerbate primitive sexual instincts - an intelligent girl should use everything for her own good.

Every strong man dreams that a woman would understand and accept him as he is, with his pros and cons. And here, for sure, a woman will need intelligence and ingenuity to be able to show a man: only she is able to make him happy.

Although there is no doubt that fools have one advantage - they have natural lightness. And it lies in their natural inability to make plans and make logical chains of inferences. These are sapience ladies who are always in tension because of the endless work of thought, trying to find a logical explanation for the actions of the opposite sex representatives, to understand what is behind this or that word of men (although men, unlike women, are straightforward), who make plans ... And the silly ones live for a day, they are able to enjoy the little things, they are undemanding - and there is their attraction.

You can often hear the advice: talk to a man on the topics that interest him. I advise you not to overdrive and not to overstrain. You should not sit and memorize how the details in his car are correctly called - do not deprive yourself of the cute charm of a gosling.

Be talkative only on the topics that are truly interesting to both of you and in which women are considered experts. It will be easy for you, and it will be informative for a man. Talk about relationships, psychology, or just a book you've read that makes you think and take a fresh look at familiar things. So you can push the man to some realizations and discoveries that may be useful for the relationship and make your conversations exciting.

Learn to ask smart, philosophical questions - when a person asks about something, it seems that he already knows the answer. And besides, the fact that you are interested in his opinion is very flattering. In order to capture a man, you must yourself be a captured person, whom one wants to follow and grow spiritually and intellectually together.

MINUTE OF WISDOM

I am a woman and it means I am an actress; there are one hundred persons and one thousand roles in me.

I am a woman and it means I'm a czarina, beloved of all the czars on earth.

I am a woman and it means I'm a slave, who got the salty taste of insults.

I am a woman and it means I'm the desert, which will incinerate you.

I am a woman; I am strong against my will, but, well, even if life is a struggle,

I am a woman, I am weak to pain, I am a woman and it means I'm a fate.

I am a woman, I am just a flash of passion, my destiny is work and patience...

I am a woman; I am that great piece of luck that nobody preserves at all

I am a woman and I am dangerous with it, fire and ice forever are in me.

I am a woman and it means I'm beautiful, from infancy until I'm old and gray.

I am a woman and all roads in the world; they lead to me, and not to any Rome.

I am a woman, I was chosen by God, although he has already punished me!

Natalya Ochkur

How to catch the fancy of a modern man? 5 new rules!

Do you go on dates but without success?

Have you read over tons of literature about the mysterious male nature, but their advice doesn't work?

Do you regularly attend women's trainings? You have both heels and gracefulness. And you seem to be doing everything right ...

You dream of meeting the Man of your Dreams, but ... for some reason you are out of luck.

Yes, a lot of modern girls dream of romantic love and try very hard to be attractive. And I am sincerely sorry that most of these efforts are wasted and they do not achieve the desired goals in Personal life.

Do not worry. Don't blame yourself!

The modern world is changing rapidly and even those "rules" that were effective only five years ago have lost their relevance!

If you are tired of facing romantic disappointments and dream of personal happiness, it's time to replace the old rules with effective NEW ones!

1. The old rule: SUPPRESS YOUR FEELINGS!
New rule: EXPRESS YOUR SYMPATHY!

Extremes are always bad. It is necessary to show your sympathy and disposition. Complete indifference to a man will inspire only emotional masochists. A man should understand that he has a real chance to make you fall in love with him. After all, no matter how beautiful and desirable Angelina Jolie is, no mentally healthy, adequate man will waste time on her conquest.

Demonstrating emotional dependence, desperately clinging to a relationship, confessing your feelings to a man who has not won your trust, respect yet, who has invested neither time nor energy in your relationship yet - means to sign a death warrant for your nascent feelings. It is VERY IMPORTANT for every girl to understand the truth: YOU should not choose your man, but make sure that this is your man! Do you feel the difference?

MINUTE OF WISDOM

The deepest, the most sincere desire is the desire to be close to someone. Further, there are reactions: a man and a woman come into play, but what precedes this - mutual attraction - is impossible to explain. This is a desire in its purest form. And while it still remains like this, the man and woman are in love with life and live every moment consciously and enthusiastically, never ceasing to wait for the right moment when it will be possible to celebrate a new blessing. They do not rush, do not hasten, do not push on the sequence of events with unconscious actions. Because they know: the inevitable will manifest itself, the truth will surely find a method and a way to reveal itself. When the time comes, they will not hesitate and will not miss it - this magical moment, because they have already learned to recognize the importance of every second.

Paulo Coelho "Eleven minutes"

2. Old rule: BE MODEST AND DO NOT SHOW YOUR INTELLIGENCE TO A MAN!

New rule: APPRECIATE and DEMONSTRATE YOUR UNIQUENESS!

A modern man needs a real person next to him for a long-term relationship, and not a dumb, evens a beautiful doll. In our turbulent time, a man needs a woman with whom he can solve life issues, consult, whose opinion he values and respects.

Men are team players, and the feeling of a secure rear will not hurt either of them. Demonstration of feigned modesty and humility will not allow all facets of your personality to manifest. But, what if you are a diamond?

3. Old Rule: MAKE HIM jealous!

New rule: MAKE HIM CONSTANTLY THINK ABOUT YOU!

When a man is in love, he concentrates on his beloved darling. All dreams, plans, thoughts are dedicated to the only one! And in order to evoke such a psychological reaction in a normal person, such an obsession with you, you need with all your might, namely with the help of female intrigue, to become interesting to him. Learn the techniques of female intrigue and the mechanisms of falling in love, train.

Jealousy is only a tiny part of today's seduction program. Besides, it's better to make him feel competitive than jealous. Competition is distinguished from jealousy by the lack of direct evidence. And besides, faithful women have always been appreciated - everyone wants to raise their own children and be sure of this.

SMILE

A woman at a psychoanalyst:

- Doctor, I have a problem! Any date ends in bed! I just can't refuse! And then I feel like such a fool and a whore, and it oppresses me terribly!

Doctor:

- Okay, now I will put you into a trance, and when you get out of it, you will be able to refuse...
Woman:
- Why "refuse" ?! Make me not feel like a fool and a whore!

4. The old rule: TAKE CARE OF HIM!
New rule: UNDERSTAND HIM!
It is not just care; it is understanding, inspiration, sympathy that modern men want. Treat him as an equal partner, but take into account the individual characteristics of male psychology. He does not need your sympathy and attitude towards him as a little one - it would rather humiliate him than tie him to you. He already has a mom! Don't try to be the second one.

It is better to be the only woman in his life who is able to support in difficult times with kindness and affection, and it will be natural for your couple, and not because the great patriarchy bequeathed this.

5. Old rule: BE INACCESSIBLE!
New rule: BE NATURAL!
If you have time - meet! You won't need to artificially create a lack of communication with you at the beginning of a relationship, and you won't have to do it if you live a colorful and interesting life. It is natural that you do not have "a boatload of time".

David Lieberman, an American researcher of human behavior, once said: "The more we communicate with someone, the more he likes us." And, indeed, the more often and longer we spend time with a potential partner, the more interested he becomes, the more he begins to like us.

Therefore, at the very beginning of the relationship, I advise you to see your young man more often and regularly, even to look for reasons for meetings on your own. But when he gets used to you and you feel that he is practically at your feet - learn to mysteriously disappear, referring to natural, and not fictitious, preoccupation. Indeed, according to the same psychologist, men love to "catch up" if a woman "escapes", and, on the contrary, men "run away" if she tries to catch up.

These, of course, are not all new rules, but some of the most important and useful if you want to attract a modern man and create an equivalent happy relationship with him.

SMILE

Women's to-do list...

To buy a lot of dresses.

Not to wear them, because jeans are more comfortable.

To buy awesome shoes to go with a dress.

To look for a fantabulous dress to go with which I bought fantabulous shoes ...

To tear tights.

To buy new ones.

To tear.

Straight hair - to curl. Curly - to straighten.

To grow your hair.

To cut hair close.

To whine that you want long hair.

To repeat the first three points.

To listen to sad songs purposely.

To work yourself up into a state

To burst into tears

To block him.

To unblock him.

To block him.

To unblock him.

To repeat these sacramental rites.

To take offense.

To wait until he apologizes.

To find out that he did not understand that you took offense.

To take offense.

To make an appointment with a friend.

To ask not to be late.

To be an hour late.

Oh, that's it...

LESSON 6

BETTER BE BORN AMBITIOUS THAN RICH.

TAKE ACTION!

The infantilism of society is especially pronounced in the sphere of personal life. We can be overactive at work, but at the same time, we categorically refuse to regularly visit "fishing spots" and learn the skills of a female pickup.

You need to understand that the old rules do not work in the modern world any more. Modesty is good, but active ones win. Choose a worthy one yourself and give him a chance to make the acquaintance of you. Remember, you just give an opportunity; the initiative of acquaintance should belong to him. At least he should be sure of that. Your task is always to be ready (both externally and internally) for a fateful meeting.

"Invisible Women". Bad advice

The Invisible Woman is perhaps the most effective style that protects us from men's attention. A woman, consciously or unconsciously, makes herself invisible for men.

For this reason she:

- dresses inconspicuously, not fashionable;
- practically does not use decorative cosmetics; rarely comes to the beautician, and then usually everything is limited to a cheap "cleansing" or "mask". She is for "natural aging" or / and she always has no money for herself;

- speaks in a low voice, as if afraid of offending or being misunderstood;

- to rare compliments usually reacts with an acute attack of modesty;

- tries to avoid being the center of attention. Even on her own birthday, she prefers to raise toasts to her parents, and not to herself;

- at a disco, corporate event, party, takes a strictly observant position.

In general, she can be anyone: a mother, a daughter, an excellent specialist, an irreplaceable office worker, a human band-aid for solving other people's problems. The main thing is that she thinks that this behavior provides her with a comfortable existence. Avoiding any active actions towards men, she seems to want to avoid the problems that they can bring. This is either an experience of an unsuccessful marriage, falling in love, or caring mommy's instructions, or in her childhood, there was a family model that was not worthy of imitation. The woman is afraid of burning her fingers again of an unhealthy relationship.

The paradox is that we often get in life what we fear and avoid the most. Often in the captivity of her modest feminine charm, men are not too self-confident, and therefore problematic. Life seems to give her confirmation of her fears. *"Have you been afraid? - take this!"*

Of course, there is another side to the coin. It is a pity that this is a medal for a "mediocre life." Pretentious appearance, catchy colors mask no worse than lifeless gray. It's like butterflies, whose bright colors also serve as a kind of protection. Too fashionable, glamorous girls arouse enthusiasm only among macho or not too sober men.

There are several more tactical tricks, "bad advice", using which you will forever forget about man affection.

- Eternal desire to be right. What do you want: to be right or to be happy? Take your pick!

- Conversation, built not as a conversation, but as a demonstration of your "valuable" knowledge, achievements, memories.

- Avoiding to look in the eye. Usually, avert your eyes.

- Do not mention the name of the interlocutor in a conversation (or even better to forget him).

- Stoneface or "myopathic face". *"Smile?! What's the point?"*

- Constant internal worries about your person. "Will I impress? And what if no! That's awful!"

- A categorical, confident tone that does not give an opportunity to object, but at the same time to relax in your company.

Demonstrating your unpretentiousness in your personal life and explaining all the failures in it by this fact, remember that you should not confuse your unpretentiousness with infantilism. It is fear and laziness that are the real sources of passivity.

Be brave! The philosopher and psychologist I. N. Kalinauskas said: *"Love is the removal of distance."* Open up your personality to others, trust and rely, do not "take cover" or "close" others for yourself and for your sincere feelings. Let the man next to you feel needed, valuable. Let him know with your communication style that you admire him. After all, we often spend so much effort to hide it. And we ourselves are waiting for understanding, adoration and love in return. Isn't it crazy?

Ask yourself what is behind your lack of self-confidence? What are you afraid of? How can this be overcome? And does your strategy for communicating with men help you achieve what you really want? And what will happen in 10 years if you don't change your approach to communication now?

We ourselves are the builders and architects of the walls of solitude around us. And only after realizing the personal contribution to their construction, you can begin to remove them. I am sure that behind them you will meet your true love and a new life, full of REAL, living, sincere, warm relationships.

SMILE
A well-mannered person will never say "Go to Jericho!...", he will say: "I see you will go far."
Female pick-up

Sometimes, when we see an attractive guy, we freeze in anticipation and hope that he will definitely take the initiative. And very often we are disappointed. What should you do in order not to miss your chance next time? Forget about old rules and get active. The most important thing is the frame of mind. You need to believe that you deserve the best and you will do a huge favor to the young man by giving him the chance to become the man of your dreams.

According to psychologist Kurt Lewin, motivation is always based on the struggle between "I want" and "I'm afraid." Even if a man really liked you, it is quite possible that he had a bad dating experience in the past. Help him to overcome his fear - hint him that you are ready to communicate with him. The main difference between a woman's pickup and a man's one: girls should not get to know the guys they like; they only create conditions for them to manifest this desire. With the help of hints, you make it clear that you are ready to hear the first words from him with a possible continuation.

The main thing is to attract attention. To do this, do the following.

Catch his eye and smile. Look at him from time to time and hold your gaze.

Demonstrate yourself. Play with your hair, gently run your fingertips over your neck, tidy hair again, and throw your head back slightly.

Get confused. As if you are ashamed of your thoughts. Ideally, if you can blush a little, it's charming. Tilt your head to one side, lower your eyes.

Remain lightly thoughtful. When you realize that he is already on the hook, take a thoughtful look aside. Your playfulness has been replaced by dreaminess or seriousness. So try, guess!

Make your movements sensual and the pose relaxed. Delicately play with a pen, fork, glass, without looking at the chosen one. Let him use his imagination.

Show that you are bored. If you seem too busy, he will not want to distract you. Demonstrate that you are free and a little bored.

If he is interested, hold your gaze. Look towards the restroom and the way there, give him one more look. It is likely that you will "accidentally" collide near the exit.

The second, more direct approach in the pickup is to start speaking to him first. It will require a little more courage from you, but learn to treat the dating process as a game - as if you are playing with a bow and a kitten.

When passing by, just say "Hello!", accidentally on purpose.

Give an innocent compliment. It should not be about his physical qualities or have sex connotation. For example: "Great tie" plus the most dizzying smile in your arsenal.

Turn to him with a request. If you are in a restaurant, ask to hand over a napkin, menu, close the window. On the street, ask for directions, ask to help with something.

Misidentify him and apologize right away charmingly. You will need acting abilities, but if you consider that all women are a bit of an actress, then it will not be difficult.

Call a friend. Ask to use the phone. You urgently need to call or write a text message, and then, by hard adventure, the phone runs out of charge - tough luck!

Accidentally sit down next to him in transport or at the airport. And then notice him and give him a warm smile.

"This is my first time here", "I don't know anyone here" are good phrases for meeting someone at an event.

Ask for advice when buying. When choosing a tie for dad, brother, wine for a party, cheese for wine - it all depends on the specialization of the trade establishment where Cupid's arrow overtook you, ask his expert opinion.

"Have we ever met?" Wait until he is alone, come and ask the question: "I see you have been watching me all evening. Have we ever met?"

So you hinted that "these eyes against him are not against." Further, the initiative passes into the hands of the man. He should have a strong impression that he was the initiator of the acquaintance. And if you've exchanged phone numbers, try not to call him first. Believe me: if a man wants to continue dating, he will definitely call you back within the next three days. Well, if not, then he missed his chance. The world is big and there are thousands of options and possibilities. One of the main laws of philosophy says: sooner or later, quantitative indicators turn into qualitative ones. Fate helps the brave!

Coach exercise "Shooting with eyes"

In front of the mirror, train to smile, to feel sad, to imitate seduction, to surprise, to joy, to get interested, to intrigue in different ways ... Choose, what smile seems to you the most attractive, what expression - the sweetest. Remember and apply!

How to make acquaintances online?

You dream of woman happiness, registered on a dating site, spent 5 minutes filling out a questionnaire, attached a couple of successful photos - and reliable, handsome and wealthy men immediately began to write to you. Confused by the choice, you finally agreed to go on a date with the most worthy, and, of course, he took you to the best restaurant. A successful, athletic, wealthy handsome man with the smile of the agent 007 greeted you with flowers, and you had a fabulous evening. He appeared to be a very attentive and emotional interlocutor, you could not stop talking, and as soon as you came back home, he called you back and thanked you for that evening. There is no doubt - you liked each other! "This is your destiny!" - the heart pounded. An invitation to a second date followed immediately, and you ran there absolutely elated. You felt: it was love at first sight! Seeing HIS eyes, you realized that the feeling was mutual. Hallelujah! Further - a sweet acquaintance with your parents, a mother-in-law in love with you, joint plans for the future ... And now you are on an exotic island, he puts you on a Cartier ring with a diamond of absolutely immodest size. You are in a luxurious champagne wedding dress from Vera Wang, and a long and happy life awaits you...

You have just read the dream scenario of all the girls who sign up on dating sites. We all want it to be that way, BUT!... In reality, usually, Hollywood stories do not work...

No, I'm not saying that this can never happen. After all, you can meet your destiny even on the way to the supermarket. Of course, it happens, but the percentage probability here is about the same as the opportunity to get rich through the lottery.

In reality, it usually happens in the following way: you register on a dating site. Different men begin to write to you, among them, there are both young fellows and old men, and, mildly speaking, vulgarians.

You have doubts about the adequacy of the homo sapiens, you are outraged by obscene proposals, disappointed by dates ... Once you meet a charming and pleasant man in all respects. You spend a wonderful evening with him, and it seems to you that this is your fate! But the next day he doesn't call back, and on the second, and on the third ... Or he calls back, and the romantic relationship continues, but then it turns out that he is not in love, and you are one of many. Your heart is broken. You will probably suffer and cry in your pillow at night. And it is logical enough that you want to curse all this online dating, delete your profile forever and give up the search.

But before you finally decide that virtual dating is not for you, find out about the top 10 mistakes that girls often make - perhaps the reason is in them? Agree, if you knew about them in advance, you could have avoided them, and your romantic search would be much more successful!

Believe me, a lot of girls make common mistakes when dating online.

Mistake # 1. Always searching for suitable sites

Imagine that your friend decided to dramatically slenderize and play sports, but still can't find a suitable gym. The locker room is uncomfortable, the coaches are unprofessional, sometimes too close, sometimes too far from home. Agree, all this is not convincing because if a person really wants something, he will find the ways. You can find good men on any website, so stop looking for the perfect one and better rethink your dating strategy.

Mistake # 2. Taking your presentation on the site lightly

Of course, you are a very attractive girl, and HE should guess about this from the fuzzy and blurry photos of last year's vacation. And HE is able to feel the depth and beauty of your soul, as well as the power of the intellect, by two or three banal lines in your profile! It's a pity, but usually, men are not so deep and do not have telepathic intuition.

If you want to achieve success, you will have to spend your time and money on beautiful and presentable photos, prepare good texts, constantly raise your profiles in the ranking for a fee, and devote enough time to correspondence.

SMILE

"Do you believe in love at first sight? " a girl asks.

"No," he answers.

"Then look at me again," she says.

Mistake # 3. Request not to disturb if candidates are undesired

You clearly know what your partner should be, and you just honestly ask the freaks, losers, alcoholics and similar types not to take up your precious time. Usually, you write: "You are more than 50 years old, you live in Turkey or you abuse alcohol - please do not write to me!" But they continue to write. What to do? Just ignore. In the end, your job is not to scare off the wrong men, but to attract those men that you like.

Mistake # 4. You expect men to write to you first.

You sit in front of the computer and wonder why only losers write to you, but the men you like passes by, and you wait for a worthy one to write. It is not customary for us if a woman takes the initiative. You don't want to seem in need of attention. But in fact, men are flattered when an attractive girl pays attention to them. And if you have cool photos and interesting text, then most men will be glad to see your attention to their person. An easy, original, meaningless phrase sent to a man you like will increase your choice.

Mistake # 5 Thinking that Great Date Will Repeat

Statistically, 50% of first dates don't have a follow-up. It is a fact and it just needs to be accepted. Even a delightful date, a pleasant time together is not a guarantee that you will meet again. And it does not mean at all that your chosen one did not like you, that there was something wrong, because there can be 1000 different reasons for this! You shouldn't think about it at all! Think of the first date as zero and the opportunity to have a good time with someone you like.

Mistake number 6. Ignoring of your own intuition

How often were you on a date with a man and caught yourself thinking that it would be better just to go to the cinema with your friend? You felt that they were lying to you, that they were trying to carry the face of someone who they really were not. Before blaming yourself for attracting some wrong men, understand that the only thing you can influence is your decisions. If you are uncomfortable with this person, trust your intuition. You should not break yourself and adapt to someone, as they say, time works wonders. You need to spend time with those people with whom you feel good and comfortable. And to have less disappointment, get to know each other better by correspondence, talk several times on the phone and listen to your internal reactions.

Mistake # 7. Looking for an ideal man

I do not argue that ideal men are probably found somewhere, and this place is inhabited by the same ideal women, but this is definitely not planet Earth. We are just people, and each person has his pros and cons. Remember that the best is the enemy of the good. And the search for the ideal is often caused by an unconscious fear of men, a kind of mind games, attempts of our subconscious mind to protect us from relationships and new disappointments.

Mistake # 8. Wishing to please everyone

This is a sure way to eternal neurosis. Even if you are Miss Universe, there is no guarantee that everyone will be your fans. And if you perceive dating sites as the final selection for a beauty contest or the show "Come on, girls!", then eternal tension and sadness are guaranteed to you. Only a light attitude towards romantic search will allow you to succeed.

Mistake # 9. Thinking that men write the truth about themselves in their profiles

Nobody likes to be deceived. And it's really unpleasant for you when a short, unshaven man comes to you on a date instead of that confident status man who smiled at you from the new Mercedes in the photo. Agree, you also sometimes belittle your age, weight, add height to yourself, expose retouched photographs, and all this seems harmless to you. And if you, an honest and decent girl, can afford it, then why can't men do the same? In my opinion, everything is fair! Men can be tempted to distort reality a little too.

Mistake # 10. Show your disinterest

"I'm not like that; I'm just waiting for a tram!" - This is a good strategy for flirting with men you already know, you have already met and who have already become attached to you and are trying to gain your favor. In virtual dating, the competition is too high, on the sites there are thousands of profiles of attractive women. And so your

"Hello! How are you? Good " will not help you attract and hold the attention of men. If you do not want to get lost among hundreds of other profiles, you must be original in your replies and messages. No one expects Hemingway's brilliant brevity or Bernard Shaw's sparkling wit from you. Be sincere, you can optimize the search process with the help of several pre-prepared template letters, where you tell in understandable language about yourself, your expectations, dreams and how the man will be lucky if he chooses you. Do not skimp the words - let the man feel your interest in him. It turns out that online dating is not the easiest way to personal happiness, and it does not provide any guarantees, but it can become a real challenge for your sense of purpose. This is a choice for really persistent, optimistic women who know what they want and believe in themselves and their destiny. In a word, it's up to you to decide how and with whom to get acquainted, whether you have enough patience and enthusiasm, you know yourself better. But according to statistics, most of the modern romantic relationships began in the virtual space. So think about it.

And be happy! May the Internet help you!

5 types of virtual macho: on which men there is no use to waste your time?

Going in search of love on the Internet, it is advisable to know who you may encounter. The world of illusions and underwater reefs-disappointments awaits you in the endless sea of online dating, if you do not approach this issue using your head.

First, you need to understand what kind of candidates you may face. So, when going for mushrooms, it is wiser to first learn everything about inedible mushrooms, so that in your basket there are no toadstools accidentally.

So, get acquainted: men-toadstools of the Internet.

Type # 1. "Pearl-fisher"

It's not for nothing that I put him first, he is good! A sort of superman of the Internet. He immediately inspires confidence and matches the image of a real man. He is attentive, regularly sends SMS, calls, tries to speed up the meeting as much as possible and amazes by his scope. He usually invites to expensive restaurants and luxury resorts. His task is to "shake you down" for love.

The novelty and sincere emotions seduce his nature, and it cannot be obtained simply for money. It's hard not to "be taken in" by such care and generosity, and very soon you start making joint plans, dreaming of quiet family evenings. But your rose and candy stage is somehow suspiciously prolonged. And you, like any woman, want certainty, and you start asking leading questions. And here the elusive halo of your mystery disappears, and interest in you falls both literally and figuratively. Men who light up quickly cool down quickly as well.

You are sad, it is more and more difficult for you to pretend joy when you meet, and gradually you become uninteresting for him. For him, online dating is a game and an opportunity to be filled with fresh feminine energy, as well as diversify his collection of women with a new exhibit for pleasant memories.

If you are looking for a partner for life, you are simply wasting time with him. Often in such "comrades" one can find serious inclinations of a narcissistic nature with all its signs. He needs lightness and emotions, and in order to find them he "dives" into the abyss of online dating. Regularly. Relentlessly.

Type # 2. "The sovereign has arrived!"

He resembles "Seeker", but everything looks a little more prosaic, he clearly knows what he wants, he is self-confident and even too much. Romantic TOURIST! His self-confidence is amazing, his inadequacy is surprising because often he is a rather shabby little man with average capabilities. But, coming to the homeland of potential brides, he sorts out candidates carefully and somehow very shamelessly.

He does not waste time on flirting, he immediately moves on to the practical side of the issue. He talks in detail about his clearly inflated claims. He considers himself a gift of fate, the difference in more than ten years does not confuse him. He is sure that he should be loved such as he is (that is, disinterestedly). You are perceived as a thing, as a person-function and, most likely, little will change over time.

Type # 3. Romantics living freely on the road

Quite simply, beggars and losers. In the questionnaire, they often write that they are looking for high and unselfish feelings. They often imagine themselves to be successful businessmen, trying to be photographed against the background of expensive cars. They amaze with the beauty of words, poetic phrases, throw virtual pictures of roses and doves, smiley kisses and other Internet rubbish. They like to talk about life, to philosophize.

They are very offended if you want specifics and real meetings. Meeting for them is exposure. And a personal meeting will not please you either: as a rule, they embellish their status, they say that post photos from the "best" times.

Be ready to pay the bill in a cafe and listen to a philosophical text about the injustice of the world, women, bosses, etc. They need Internet dating to feed their wounded ego, to justify their own laziness. They really hope to somehow get the attention of inexperienced women who will believe their fables about temporary difficulties and high and unselfish feelings. This is an eternal prince. And he will never become a king. It's hopeless!

Type # 4. Lovers of the adult movie

His task is to trick you into sex on Skype or just a demonstration of your charms. The porn, which is abundant on the Internet, no longer suits them. They are aroused, so to say, by the live broadcast. Remember: whatever the schemes of these dodgers are, sex presupposes the active participation of two people in love, and it is preceded by a period of courtship, which means efforts from the man's side. Do not trust promises, do not fall into the trap like "Show that you trust me" or "Be sexier, more liberated."

Never agree on virtual sex with a man who has not done anything yet to meet and conquer you in real life. A person who respects you and himself will not extort erotic broadcasts. Take care of your reputation!

By the way, women told me several cases when not only their reputation suffered, but also their wallet. Some virtual perverts are also blackmailers.

Type # 5. Knight "Wounded Heart"

He recently broke up with a girlfriend or wife and is ready to find love again. It's just very strange that most of the time he talks about his ex, whom he is struggling to forget. And more and more often you remind yourself of a "shoulder", if not more - "a place for emotional waste." Yes, surviving a breakup is not easy, but you need to go to specialists or friends, and not use fragile female souls.

Scientists have found that it takes about 17 months to forget a former love. Only after this period a person is able to build new happy relationships. Usually, romantic relationships that started during this period end with disappointment for a new passion. You don't have to become a love pill. Well, you really deserve more. You need your own real relationship, not the pale ghosts of his past in your destiny.

Perhaps I have not told you about all types of "Internet toadstools", the virtual world is huge and diverse. But now you know about the brightest representatives, about the most "poisonous" ones.

Remember, you are not a cheap emotional store for irresponsible men and not an object in the house for an old stranger, not a personal porn star for perverts and not a psychotherapist for all "humiliated and abused".

You are a woman worthy of Love! And your relationship should be tasty and healthy.

Coach exercise "100 fans"

Excessive demands are as dangerous as carelessness about choosing a life partner. And everything in its own time: at the first stage of the search, do not try to find an ideal husband (after all, you have not lost him), but rather set a goal for yourself to understand your tastes and needs, better understand men and feel what kind of men brings you positive emotions and comfort, and which of them are unpleasant. Start going on a date for a check mark to complete your 100 Dating plan.

This goal is more sustainable in relation to yourself, it allows you to know yourself better and does not lead to disappointments. Chat with different men who don't even match your ideal visualizations, develop your own experience by tracking your impressions. From time to time ask yourself the following questions:

-What kind of men are annoying?
- What exactly do you dislike?
- What do men that you like have in common?
- What can you get from them?
- What can you give in return?

LESSON 7

TAKE FAILURES LIGHTLY!
LEARN FROM THEM AND JUST MOVE ON.
QUANTITY ALWAYS TURNS INTO QUALITY.

In our turbulent times, we are afraid to fall in love. We are afraid of getting caught in this addiction and thus disrupting the relative comfort of our usual life.

And some of us have open mental wounds after the recent "love victories". New disappointments are frightening.

But what if it's time to love? There is one great and reliable way to bring romantic enthusiasm back into your life - to fall in love intelligently, using your head. I would even say, for convenience, but, as the heroine Udovichenko said in the movie "The Most Charming and Attractive", the main thing is that the convenience is correct.

Ask yourself the question: what are you counting on? What will bring a bright feeling of love to your destiny? And why is it so important for you? Which man is convenient for you?

Why do the men who happen to be around, not linger?

Ania will be my client today, and this is our first coaching session. She came in all so cheerful, excessively talkative and friendly, beautiful, I would even say flawless, a winner. Everything in her spoke about success. In a career. She refused coffee, it was predictable: the policy of not making people the slightest inconvenience is characteristic of patient excellent pupils. After 10 minutes of the session, she was already crying, although I asked only a few leading questions. It was loneliness trying to break out.

Like stone walls, facades of external well-being of such as Ania, collapse during consultations of psychologists and coaches.

Why does it so often happen that successful women find themselves defenseless in love relationships?

There are many men around them, they look great, but the fans don't stay long. At some point, the fear of being alone prevails over the crazy fun of youth. And they begin to grab at a straw of pseudo-teachings of various women's trainings, which, interrupting each other, offer to open chakras in all decent and indecent places, to learn to play a magic pipe, to become a goddess, a bitch, an angel. Finally confused, they start looking for new ways or give up.

Fortunately, it is enough to explain to the owners of a strong intellect how the system works, the basic laws of life, so that they re-understand their behavior and philosophy and stop living on the machine of their usual reactions.

How to use the two main rules of the universe in your personal life: the law of reflection and likeness, where "the outside reflects the inside" and "like sees like"?

In any person, there is a dad and a mom, where dad is the woman's internal programs, and mom is her external programs. And almost all the difficulties in relationships with men arise from problems with parents in childhood.

In an ideal childhood, a girl looks at her father as an innovator, founder, creator of life, a "giver", someone who teaches system, logic, and order. And she looks at mom as at a wise keeper - "bereginya", the one who continues and preserves the traditions of the family, cares, gives warmth, affection, happiness, and does it all with pleasure.

A woman's external success is determined by her mother's behavior in childhood. By copying it, the woman learns how to behave. Thanks to him, a woman will interact with society. If a mother did not demonstrate love and care for herself, her husband, family, daughter, then a woman in adulthood will show the same skills. If the mother did not show affection and tenderness, then the adult "girl" also will not know how to do it.

For the sake of truth, it is worth saying that there is another unconscious external behavioral scenario, when a girl anticopies the mother's behavior, becomes her external opposite - the reason for this is her childhood love for her dad, the so-called Electra complex (jealousy of the mother, protest against the mother).

The consequence of relationships with dad in childhood is a program of love or animus towards herself, internal acceptance of herself as she is, attitude towards men, and the attitude of men towards her. The girl learns to believe men and in men.

For example, if dad "betrayed", it is in such a way the child often perceives the divorce of the parents or father's unfaithfulness, then even in adulthood, it will be difficult for her to build open, sincere relationships. And if her mother was also hysterical or emotionally cold, then she would not even be able to talentedly play "affinity". A woman has neither an internal nor an external scenario of happiness.

In personal relationships, we attract men with the external (attractiveness), and we keep them with the internal (inner beauty). Therefore, beautiful women are surrounded by attention, but often the general situation in their personal life is unfavorable, and this is a consequence of internal children's complexes.

On a subconscious level, people know absolutely everything about each other, and there are no random situations. All so-called accidents are subconscious patterns. Therefore, the internal dragons of self-doubt, self-rejection attract ugly relationships.

We do not love ourselves as we are, we are all trying to play somebody without any show of talent, and we are not loved as we are. And we find and attract those people who like puzzles, so fit our inner states, convictions, and beliefs, sincere desires (very often unconscious).

This is how we agree for the familiar instead of the happy.

SMILE
- If not you, - the wife sighed, - we would be a perfect couple.

MINUTE OF WISDOM
Your vision will become clear only if you can look into your heart. Those who look outward see only dreams.
Carl Gustav Jung

MINUTE OF WISDOM
I am not what happened to me, I am what I decided to become.

Carl Gustav Jung
What to do?

Sit down and make 2 lists: "What did I like about parents? What did I dislike?"

Write about personal characteristics, and about the attitude towards you, about the situation in the family. Remember in what situations and how mom behaved. Think about your behavior. How differently can you react in your usual situations? Did your father love you? Did you trust him? How did this affect your female destiny? What conclusions, understandings, decisions have you come to?

Only our conscious work towards change, our awareness, will help not to copy the mother's behavior and stop deserving love. And when we fully realize the negative impact of the child's script on our life, we decide to change our fate - only then we have a real chance to change the course of our life history. If we do not realize this, then we will simply follow the program, and, accordingly, we will not get the results we planned.

Coach exercise "Box of Happiness"

Imagine that your good mood is a pearl necklace, which at the moment of severe stress tore and crumbled along the bottom of an abandoned lake. And now you need to dive after it and catch each pearl, clean it and put it in a chic box to get it out when you need it.

Pearls are your pleasant memories, your resource.

1. Remember the best moments of your life when you felt happy, joyful and / or when you were full of optimism, sweet anticipation.

Allow yourself to return mentally to the joyous moment. What did you feel then? If there was a place in your body for this feeling, where would it be? What if this feeling had color, temperature, texture? If there was an image of this feeling, what would it be? Take a deep breath. Remember these feelings.

What will change in your soul if you take these moments and sensations with you for the next few days?

2. For 3 days, put a reminder on your phone, and every half hour recreate these images and sensations in your body, taking a deep breath. And at the same time, notice and note for yourself what is beautiful and pleasant that you see, hear, feel at the moment. This is how, bit by bit, by bead, you will regain your good mood again.

How to get rid of past relations

It just so happens in life that not all stories end with a happy ending. And many - fortunately. Each separation has its own story. People separate because of antipathy. Because of stupidity. Because of insults. Men can leave even the woman they love when their ego suffers. Women, when they love, usually do not leave. They pray. They make scenes. They tolerate. And they are waiting for a Miracle!

The rupture of relations is always very painful. All abandoned lovers (ough, what a disgusting word! Akhmatova's words come to mind: "Abandoned! An invented word. Am I a flower or a letter?") experience 2 bright post-periods.

The 1st period "Denial" - you just do not believe that this is the end. You hope that he will change his mind. You take offense, you forgive. You try not to call, you call. You are angry, you cry. You constantly analyze the relationship, you talk only about him. You return to the places where you felt good as if you can find the lost puzzles of your happiness there. You visit mutual acquaintances in an attempt to "accidentally" meet him. You re-read the correspondence, conduct mental dialogues with him. You annoy your friends with your effusions. You look at your photos, tear them to shreds, glue them together. You build with your friends or specialists of all stripes strategies for returning your loved one, then you try to prove to yourself that you are right and are worth something - and start new romantic relations. You are trying diligently to kindle the embers of his feelings, to return him at any cost ... You have a lot of energy that you ingloriously burn in the fire of empty hopes. Often you do frankly stupid things, although your brain helpfully finds an explanation and justification for each of them. It is difficult to reproach you for inaction and at the same time for adequacy. This is a period of struggle with yourself, with the past, with reality.

But one day a moment comes and you suddenly realize that everything is in vain. And then the bitter part of the love story begins - "Humility".

This is the 2nd period of your love tragedy. "Chef! Everything is lost!" - your tired brain gives the command. And the energy-saving mode turns on: universal sadness covers you. You do not try to change your fate any more. You show your former lover your powerlessness and deep despair. You are in pain, and pain is always a signal to others that you need help.

You don't seem to be hoping for anything anymore, although in reality you are using your last ace up your sleeve: you appeal to pity. Renowned anthropologist Helen Fisher explains this behavior by the fact that people are very social. Well, a person cannot calmly look at a suffering person (especially if he was once dear) - he tries to help him. Nature has programmed us to be sympathetic, otherwise, without mutual support, we would have died out at the dawn of humanity. Because of a sense of empathy, even a person who has stopped loving can return, he is not a beast, after all! But pity is not able to last long. Are you really sure that this is all that you deserve in this one life of yours? After all, if he descends, then you will return to the same relationship, to the same person, to the same problems as before.

Of course, there are interrupted romantic relations that are filled with love and meaning again. But this happens if, during the time of separation, a mutual burning desire to start all over again has appeared without strain and emotional pressure from one of the parties, when the partners realized their mistakes and decided to correct them. A relationship can be started all over again, but they shouldn't be continued.

One-way traffic in Love leads to collapse, no matter how good your intentions to make a man happy are. Accept the separation as a fact and do not try to bring him to reason or arouse compassion. Your hyper-initiative can only push him away.

"Love cannot be bought!" - you need to say this to your beloved and leave loving. Disappear from his life, despite the predictable desire to return everything at any cost. Imagine that he flew to Mars, forever. What would you do then? Try to live happily, become valuable in your eyes. Give yourself back your love, energy and respect bit by bit.

Make plans without him, paint the bright prospects of the beautiful far away. But the goals that you set for yourself should be short-term and easily achievable. Praise yourself for the smallest successes, celebrate the smallest victories.

Give yourself time. If within a maximum of a year and a half he did not return, then his decision was final. Although a few weeks of your indifference is enough for him to start worrying. Hurt self-esteem contributes to the awareness of loss.

A loving person will definitely want to return. And if he asks to be back, don't throw yourself on his neck right away, because if during the time of separation you worked a lot on yourself, you became wiser and began to truly respect and love yourself. Has he changed? Are you ready to start a relationship with this person? Start rather than continue?

SMILE

Foolish little girl! Well, why are you worried that your breast is the first size !? Instead, your shoe size is... forty-fourth!

MINUTE OF WISDOM

Now that we have learned to fly in the air like birds and dive in the sea like fish, only one thing remains - to learn to live on earth like humans.
Bernard Show

Forget the role of the victim - and forward to a wonderful future

Sometimes our past gets in the way of starting a new relationship. In the dusty closet of memory, grievances against men, unfinished romantic relations and fragments of our hearts are stored. It is not easy to live with such baggage, and to fall in love - all the more. Of course, you can continue to revel in self-pity, again there will always be gorgeous topics for conversation with pseudo-friends, but I really hope that you are reading these lines in order to find a real way out of this situation. In general, try not to fall into the viscous networks of unhappy relationships, and if you are looking for someone to live with him happily ever after, choose a person without past love disappointments. It is very difficult for a person with a sad emotional experience to remove the panic button "Hit and run!" and truly discover himself and believe.

Unfortunately, love is rare, and mutual love is even rarer. We fall in love, we suffer and think that this is normal. But this is not the case. True love is always mutual. It was conceived by nature as a unifying factor for two, it is an integral part of human happiness and is needed for joy and development.

Life is fair, and it always strives to take away from us the source of suffering - the man who caused it. Cool down and analyze the situation. Maybe it's for the best that you broke up? And, probably, in a year you will look back at this situation and smile.

In the meantime ... When we are abandoned or they say that have fallen out of love, the situation gets out of control. The whole world calms down and stops, turning into monotonous thoughts about a loved one. Unrequited love is a toothache of the soul. Often we try to return his feelings with tears, pity, reproaches - and this is the most destructive and wrong behavior. In a romantic stupor, it is difficult to turn on the brain, but only this will save you.

For unknown reasons, we cling to the side of a sinking ship in the hope that it might someday float, wasting the remaining nerves, time, and money on it.

Of course, if you take into account the prescription "perseverance wins," you must be persistent and not give up. And in this case, set the exact deadlines for achieving the goals: how long are you ready to wait?

But he does not appear, then understand the ancient Indian proverb: *"If the horse is dead - dismount."*

It's time to open your eyes and take a close look at him and yourself. Erase the pink coating of illusion from the glasses through which you look at the world. You try to bring him back in the hope that everything will change - he will suddenly realize that he is in love, he will return and begin to behave differently. It is not true! Even if he returns, he will very soon be the same as before. By the way, think about it: how much do you need a person who betrayed your love? It is better to endure a little so that, after realizing the experience gained, start from scratch with a person who is as interested in your relationship as you are. Better yet, more than you are.

Treat the process of "falling out of love" as a recovery. Yes, bitter medicine. Yes, inconvenience. Yes, you feel bad. But you know that very soon you will enter your usual life with renewed vigor. *A person is always stronger than circumstances!*

I am personally deeply sure that if he left you, you wanted it yourself. Because in nature, a woman chooses a man and gives him a chance. And if he is not with you, then, most likely, some subconscious defense mechanisms activated, your intuition saved you from unpleasant consequences. In fact, you felt that he was not yours, but you tried to cling to him. Ask yourself: why? Why was it important for you to stay with him? For what? And use these answers to shape your goals. Answer yourself to the question: how can you get all this without him? And direct your energies towards achievement!

If we talk about universal advice, then there are two of them. To forget a person as soon as possible, you need:

1) stop seeing and communicating with him;

2) try to give yourself what you received from him or hoped to receive. Plus, you can use various additional measures.

Love is, first of all, a strong self-hypnosis and fixation on the only one. Stop mentally communicating with him, thinking about him and fantasizing about a failed happy future. It was you yourself who once endowed your beloved with all possible and impossible positive qualities, and he acquired the status of super significant.

Remember all your grievances, all his shortcomings, make a list and re-read it often. If you wish, you can find a bunch of shortcomings in each - so look for. Answer the questions for yourself: did he show tenderness, hugged, gave gifts? Was it interesting and reliable with him? What real, not imagined, prospects awaited you with him? And the most important, were you happy with him or were you just hoping that he would change? Be honest with yourself!

Give your beloved some funny humiliating nickname, for example: "Fatty mcnasty", "Baldy bean", "Jelly-belly". Buy a very scary stuffed toy and call it that name. According to Japanese psychologists, this technique can reduce the importance of a person in your eyes.

Do not try to dull the pain at first. Arrange a farewell to love, buy champagne, watch melodramas, listen to chanson, invite your best friend and tell her everything - throw out your emotions. Cry - let the slags come out of the brain. Grieve to the full, don't restrain yourself until you feel better.

Get creative: sculpt, draw, write poetry and sentimental letters to him. You don't need to send them - you can read them to a friend or a psychologist who should be contacted. Go on dates, but not in order to find a replacement or a serious relationship, just for distraction and entertainment. Meet without interest, do not try to please: for you a date is just a reason to get on in the world. You will be surprised, but just when a woman stops trying hard to please and gratify everyone, she gets fans and admirers. And her own fan club hasn't hurt any girl yet.

To stop loving a man who did not love you means finally to love yourself! Take a vacation, become selfish for a while. Do what you've dreamed of for a long time, but didn't have enough time for. Now there is a great reason for self-improvement. Always remember that the darkest hour is that before the dawn. And the next man will be better than the previous one. Now you need to believe this and convince yourself of this. In the end, this will happen! You now have a lot of energy, even if negative, - sublimate it for new achievements, make plans. ***Despair is the best springboard for achievements.***

Just imagine his face when he meets you and sees that you are slim, successful, happy and with a new gentleman. You will want to say to him: "How are you, dear? Have you kicked yourself? Has it been painful?"

And remember forever: love only those who love you.

SMILE

A baby camel asks its mother:

- Mom, why do we have two such interesting humps?

- Well, we are "ships of the desert", sonny. We need them in order not to experience hunger and thirst in the desert.

- Mom, why do we have such interesting legs?

- We're "ships of the desert", sonny. We need them in order to move along the sand without experiencing difficulties.

- Mom, why do we have such a very thick coat?

- We're "ships of the desert", sonny. We need it in order not to feel hot during the day, and not to feel cold at night in the desert.

The baby camel thought, thought, and then it says:

- Mom, listen, well, I can't understand one thing! Why do we need all these bells and whistles at the zoo?!

MINUTE OF WISDOM
Knowing your own darkness is the best method for dealing with the darknesses of other people.
Carl Gustav Jung

SMILE
Building. Commission. Acceptance of work.
The taskmaster tells how excellent their order is. Suddenly a wall of the building breaks down.
The taskmaster:
- 10:44. Right on schedule.

MINUTE OF WISDOM
Decline starts with the replacement of dreams with memories and ends with the replacement of memories with other memories.
Nassim Taleb

Coach exercise "Red flags in relationships"
Determine what actions of men you consider unacceptable.
Continue phrases:

I am alarmed by men who ...

_____

_____

A real man will never allow ...

_____

_____

From now on, in communicating with me, I forbid a man ...

_____

_____

Find 3-7 variants of continuation of each phrase. Create your own rules - it makes life easier.

INFORMATION FOR REFLECTION

The ancient wisdom of the Dakota Indian tribe says that if you find yourself riding a dead horse, the best strategy is to jump off it.

It would seem that everything is clear.

However, we often try to use other strategies with the dead horse.

We try to persuade ourselves that there is still hope.

We hit the horse harder.

We're trying to feed it.

We say: "We always rode like this."

We organize a dead horse revival event.

We explain that our dead horse is much "better, faster and cheaper."

We organize a comparison of different dead horses.

We sit next to the horse and persuade it not to be dead.

We change the requirements for a horse by declaring that this horse is not dead.

We buy products that help ride faster on dead horses.

We change the criteria for identifying dead horses.

We visit other places to see how they ride dead horses there.

We take courses to develop horse management skills.

We gather colleagues to analyze a dead horse.

We are hiring dead horse specialists.

LESSON 8

A RELATIONSHIP IS NOT A GOAL IN ITSELF, BUT A PROCESS. ENJOY THE PROCESS!

You want to love and to be loved! Your wish is great! Just remember that love is not a goddess to be worshiped. "Love is a child of freedom," as one old French song says. If you suffer in a relationship, then you started it with the "wrong" person.

Nine romantic rules for a fabulous first date

As a LoveQ coach, I very often hear from my clients: "What happened? It all started so well ... He booked a table in a nice restaurant, was so attentive, we had a great time ... Where did he disappear after the first date? He never called back ... What's wrong with me? " If this is familiar to you, perhaps you simply were not guided by the main rules of a fabulous first date, which will definitely be followed by a second, third and others. In order not to make the first date the last, you need to take on board a few tips.

Tip 1. Show your interest.
The main rule of flirting: find something interesting in another!
Compliment. Just your praises for a man should be different from those that are pleasant to a girl. Praise his taste: thank him for the excellent choice of a cafe or restaurant, note his perfect tie, his gallantry. Look up to par - this is also a compliment to a man, because you did your best for him. Ask for advice on food and drink choices and he will feel significant. In general, give his ego a light massage with soft paws. Men love it.

Tip 2. Do not drink alcoholic beverages.

Of course, you won't become a kid, but you can spoil the impression of yourself. One or two glasses of champagne with juice, white wine with water - and you will not lose control of the situation. Sobriety is necessary for properly assessing a fan candidate.

Tip 3. Don't open up.

A man is not obliged to listen to heartbreaking stories about your failures, problems, difficulties in communicating with the opposite sex, about childhood burdened by the presence of "wooden toys", and so on. Stop! You are not in a psychotherapy session, and you should not turn your soul inside out. Believe me, he will not appreciate such "sincerity", but rather decide that you are another young lady with a bunch of problems. While a man is not yet over head and ears in love, he does not need your problems.

Tip 4. Don't talk about your ex.

Try not to turn the first date into a meeting of veterans of love, do not ask about his ex. When asked about the past, answer very composedly - like, yes, there was a relationship, we turned out to be different people, it sometimes happens. And there you are! Don't develop the topic. And, most importantly, you must have temporary female amnesia - do not mention aloud more than one, maximum two partners from your romantic practice.

Tip 5. Be self-confident.

Do not tell him how difficult it is for you to constantly struggle with excess weight, and at the same time with increased hairiness and sweating. Don't pay his attention to your shortcomings, don't direct his attention where you don't need to. It is better to say good about yourself, scold your merits, beautifully and subtly advertise yourself as the best offer possible. The source will be forgotten - the information will be preserved, and the impression of the first date will remain with him for life.

Tip 6. Intrigue.

Try to answer the questions about you in such a way that a man has additional questions and interest. For example, he asks about your work, you should not answer immediately and curtly: "At the bank." It's better to answer: "I make people happy and rich" (in the loan department). You are unusual, not like the others! A guy after a date should have more questions than answers. It's easy to keep his interest if you are an "unread book".

Tip 7. Listen more, talk less.

Where silence is golden, it's on the first date. You will make a good impression with your attentiveness to his story about himself rather than your talkativeness. Let the man set topics for conversation - do not look for them yourself. (Flirt idea: You can download the coaching questions on the Internet and remake them in your own way.) And don't be afraid of pauses, behave naturally: smile softly, proceed to your meal, just relax.

Tip 8. Don't make plans.

Don't ask where you will go the second time, the third, or where you will go for a romantic weekend. Even if you realized that he is the man of your dreams, do not plan anything in advance. The first meeting is considered date zero - you don't owe each other anything. Let him decide for himself how to surprise you on the first or second date, and whether he wants a new meeting. Therefore, do not call after the meeting and do not send an SMS with gratitude for a pleasant time. Just show the young man that you are very pleased to be in his company. Remember: **women's initiative kills relationships.**

Tip 9. Finish the date first.

Leave 15 minutes before you get bored. Better "under" than "over". It is better not to lengthen the first date for more than one and a half or two hours. Just express your gratitude for the aromatic coffee or a wonderful dinner (even better if it is lunch) and say that you have to go. "The shorter the parting, the less tears!" Do not start making excuses, do not sum up the results of the meeting (I liked/disliked you - You liked/disliked me).

The main thing is that the first date should be fun and easy, and then he will definitely call again.

By the way, if you felt inner tension on the first date, then this person is not suitable for you. Usually, the first impression is dictated by our unconscious, and it is difficult to deceive it.

SMILE

- Okay, young gentleman. I'll let my daughter go on a date with you. But remember: my girl was brought up under strict rules. She must return home no later than in three days.

MINUTE OF WISDOM
It is the woman who chooses the man who will choose her.
Paul Geraldi, French writer
Love hack for dating

Learn to admire a man. When he sits opposite, mentally note all the good things that you notice in him, in detail. He will definitely feel it, and the atmosphere will become magical.
Coach exercise "Intrigue"

Come up with memorable intriguing answers to his questions in advance, be creative. The main thing is that they should not be banal.

What is your job?
Your answer:

_____

_____

What do you do?
Your answer:

_____

_____

What do you like?
Your answer:

_____

_____

Tell me something interesting about yourself.
Your answer:

_____

_____

Where did you study?
Your answer:

_____

_____

What movies do you watch?
Your answer:

_____

_____

How to be an interesting interlocutor for a man

My clients often ask how to be an interesting interlocutor for a man. The answer is simple: ask questions and learn to listen to the answer with interest. The question has an amazing property of concentrating the brain in the direction of the answer, it launches such a mental search engine. It means that attention is concentrated, firstly, on the topic of the conversation, and secondly, on the individuality of the person who asked the question, because, before answering, we subconsciously evaluate who we will answer. In the first case, you need to direct your thought in the right direction for you. For example, if you want to be a "holiday for a man" - talk to him about the holidays, if you want relationships, love - talk to him about love. And it's better to ask. Don't be afraid to seem too curious - people like talking about themselves and remembering pleasant things. And let his interest and attention, the received pleasant emotions connect in his mind with your person - this will benefit your relationship.

The second benefit of asking questions is information that you can use to understand whether you need such a partner or not. By the way, try to pay attention not only to what your partner is saying, but also to how he speaks. In fact, a person often tells a lot about himself - we simply do not want or do not know how to analyze information, we prefer to live in illusions, we are concentrated on our person during the dialogue. Although, elementary attentiveness could prevent small griefs and tragedies in our personal life.

The best time for questions is the period of flirting, courtship. This is the time of the very beginning of the relationship, when it is better to keep your ears open, and not to rush to open your heart to a stranger. Ask with a grain of childlike spontaneity, sometimes in a joking tone, lightly - and analyze. Get to know him better with the prepared questions, which you can simply choose from the collection published below, and learn the basics of active listening. We like people who talk to us about us.

Coach exercise "Interesting personality"

Let's check it out with questions.

What is your favorite book? Why is it worth reading?

_____

_____

What is your favorite movie? Why is it worth watching? What aphorisms, statements have you remembered? How have they influenced your life?

_____

_____

What are your favorite parables, legends?

_____

_____

What are your signature dishes?

_____

_____

What are your favorite anecdotes?

_____

_____

What kind of music do you listen to?

_____

_____

A couple of interesting stories that happened to you in your life ...

_____

_____

MINUTE OF WISDOM

If you love without causing reciprocity, i.e. your love as love does not give rise to reciprocal love, if by your life manifestation as a loving person you do not make yourself a loved person, then your love is powerless, and it is a misfortune.

Erich Fromm, German psychologist

37 questions for a perfect date

Have you ever had any dates in your life, after which He did not call back? How often have you talked too much about yourself in an effort to impress? What if the fairy godmother gave you the recipe for the perfect date?

Yes! A date is a start, a great chance to start a lifelong relationship or ... ruin everything.

We worry before a date, like before an exam, but this is really a test of your charm and attractiveness. Whether you can withstand it with dignity or not depends on you, your chosen one, and circumstances.

Anyhow, you should do everything in your power to make the date interesting. And, perhaps, it will be the beginning of your new happy romantic story.

It is much easier to become an interesting interlocutor than it seems to be.

Ask interesting questions and practice active listening.

- I wonder what the difference between life and existence is.
- If you were an animal, what would you be?
- If you could become your own friend, would you like to have such a friend for yourself? And why?
- What does it mean for you to live with pleasure?
- What famous woman would you like to have a love relationship with?
- Describe the ideal relationship. Ideal marriage. How is the day for such couples?
- I wonder by what signs a woman can find out that a man likes her.
- What is "freedom" for you?
- I wonder how a man understands that a woman likes him.
- Do you consider yourself a romantic? What's your favorite love story?
- What is love? What is just sympathy?
- What is the difference between life and existence?
- Do you think your childhood was happier than other children's? Would you like to have the same relationship in your family as in your parents' family was?
- If you knew that you have a year left to live, what would you do? What would you change?
- What do we have in common? Start 5 sentences with "We ..."
- If you changed your gender at least for a day, who would you like to become? What would you do?
- I wonder what a man is looking for in a woman first of all.
- What is your vision of the ideal man/woman?
- What important conclusion have you made from your past relationship?
- Can you be happy only because your partner is happy? What makes you happy?
- How would you like your partner to show his love?
- Should there be a law punishing unfaithful lovers?
- Why do people try to change each other?
- What kind of people do you like?

- Describe your feelings when you fell in love first.

- Name two qualities of the opposite sex representatives that do not attract you. What attracts you?

- About whom can you say that she is "the love of my life"? What did you value most about her? What made her different from others? When was the relationship perfectly happy?

-What three things do you like to do with your partner?

- How would you like your partner to show his love?

- What does start a fire in you and what does extinguish it?

- Choosing from everyone in the world, who would you invite to dinner?

- How do you imagine a perfect day?

- If a crystal ball could tell the truth about you, your life, your future, or anything else, what would you like to know?

- What is the greatest achievement of your life?

- What is your sweetest memory?

- I wonder what the best thing you did for your woman.

SMILE

Katya picks up the phone and hears:

- Katya, is that you?

- Yes.

- Katya, excuse me, on the last date I behaved so rudely with you, pounced like an animal ... In fact, I am not like that. I beg you, forgive me, Katya! Come tonight! Give me another chance!

- Ok, I forgive you. But who is this?

Advice:

Do not ask more than 3 questions from the list on one date; do not turn it into an interrogation or a psychotherapy session. Remember that all questions must be asked playfully, lightly, with humor.

Result:

A recommendation question will reduce date anxiety and greatly increase your chances of success! Well, information rules the world!

Listen carefully and draw conclusions ...

INFORMATION FOR REFLECTION

Everything you need to know about flirting

Simple and effective advice from the main character of the film "The Naked Truth" is an excellent guide for those women who don't know how to meet an interesting man. Perhaps these recommendations will seem controversial to someone, but this is, so to speak, the naked truth, without cuts.

1. Listen, ladies! I will say it only once. And these are just four words: "WE ARE VERY SIMPLE!" We are not amenable to training. Nonsense about men from Mars is a waste of your time and money. If you want to stay lonely - it's your right! Read the waste paper. But, if you need relationships, then the only way to them is - get on the fitness machines, lose weight! Take care of yourself and at the same time buy some sexy lingerie. After all, all of us are interested only in forms!

2. You met a handsome, intelligent and self-sufficient guy, you really liked him, and you even exchanged phone numbers, but he does not call. What to do? Call yourself or wait? Perhaps he is very busy, or he is in trouble, or he just lost your business card. How do you know what really happened? After some time, you can call him first, demand nothing, not curry favor, just ask some supposedly important question. Speak briefly and to the point, as soon as the conversation has exhausted itself, say goodbye and hang up.

3. Be unpredictable, be a riddle addicted, busy with something or someone, independent, etc.

4. No criticism of men, even constructive ones. If you want to point out mistakes, make him decide on the right actions himself, direct him imperceptibly and unobtrusively.

5. Be cheerful - men appreciate it.

6. Men love with their eyes, so it's time to change your wardrobe - change inaccessibility to "I want you".

7. At the early stages of dating, in no case talk about your problems - you will look like a bore in the eyes of a man.

8. You must combine ice and fire in yourself - be inaccessible and cold and at the same time beckoning with your sexuality of a stripper.

A bitch is outside, a nymphomaniac is inside.

9. Know how to turn down for a while, but keep him on a hook. The longer he asks, the deeper the hook sticks...

10. Simulate an orgasm if necessary. Do it with enthusiasm, and then playing orgasm will bring you pleasure.

Ten tips for making a man fall in love with you

The good news is that you don't have to change dramatically in order to make a man fall in love with you. On the contrary, you must remain yourself, live your life, be a person. The only thing you need is to change your behavior a little and follow a few simple tips.

INFORMATION FOR REFLECTION

According to the principles of neurolinguistic programming in communication, the meaning of a sent message is not the intention behind the message, but the kind of reaction it provokes.

1. Try to look seductive.

Men love with their eyes. Remember this first rule as "Our Father": in order for you to be courted, you must take care of yourself. A slim figure, shiny hair, stylish clothes, a seductive scent of perfume - you should look so that all the men around you want you. Let them admire, let them keep their eyes on you - this will only add attractiveness to you. He will be proud that there is such a beauty nearby and he managed to win her attention from other potential gentlemen. A man likes to feel like a winner.

2. Be conversable and smile.

Smiling is disarming - one more commonplace to use when seducing. It should be easy and pleasant for a man to be in your company, then he will love this state and strive for it. If you are interesting for the object of desire, he will try to make a lasting impression. So show that he did it! Be free, laugh at his jokes, even if you've heard them before. Laughter, a flirtatious smile, a pleasing look - all this will be direct evidence that you are having a great time in his company. We fall in love with those people who make us believe that we are the best.

3. Be polite and nice.

Cynicism, arrogance, rudeness - all this is not about you. If you are rude to the waiter, the man will think that this is just the tip of the iceberg and that there will be more! Of course, you have to show that you have principles, but not in the form of arrogance - otherwise, you will remain alone forever.

4. Find out what he dreams of and be interested in his hobbies.

Nice, flirty, light conversations are cool, but sometimes too boring. Talk from time to time on serious and interesting topics for him: about plans, ambitions, dreams. They say that the scale of the personality is determined by the quality and the globality of his dream. So believe in a man's dream and inspire him to accomplishments! Even if today it seems impossible, the beloved will feel that you believe in his dreams, and therefore in him. Try to make man's intellect fall in love with you: if he is captured by something, something causes him passion - let him speak. And this inspired state will always be associated with you.

SMILE
- Am I fat?
- No, you aren't.
- But losing weight wouldn't go amiss, right?
- I like you like that.
- But I do not cause delight, right?
- You cause delight.
- But not rabid, right?..

5. Watch with acute fascination.

He should feel irresistible in your presence. Studies have shown that lovers look at each other 80% of the time. During a conversation, look directly into his eyes, as if trying to perceive his soul, read his thoughts. As soon as your eyes meet, hold your gaze - let it be meaningful and give hope, make you fantasize, dream ... People fall in love with their illusions.

6. Touch gently.

Accidentally on purpose touch him. And once again ... With all the tenderness that you are only capable of. Take sensory memory as your ally, his body will remember these light excitements in your presence. Take his hand when crossing the road, hug him a little more gently when you meet, touch when communicating, wear clothes made of fabrics agreeable to the touch: sliding silk, fur ... Tactile sensations are very important for confirming your own attractiveness. And you already know that a man should feel amazing in your presence.

7. Showcase your talents.

If you want to make a man fall in love, then you must understand how to surprise him with your talent: come up with ways, be creative. He may think he knows you well, but always leave room for a surprise. Men appreciate novelty and love to explore everything, so may they not to get tired of getting to know you. If you are of a captured nature, it will be easier for you to captivate a man as well. Give him a chance to see your talents and admire himself once again - because he has been able to attract the attention of such an extraordinary girl like you.

MINUTE OF WISDOM

Love is like a Louis Vuitton bag: it's either genuine or you don't need it. Author is unknown

8. Don't be easily accessible.

Of course, it's hard to be an ice maiden when you are in love. But this is how a person is made - we value only what is difficult to get. As soon as you understand that you aroused the man's interest, try to limit the time of communication with him. Be friendly, sweet, but from time to time cancel meetings because of circumstances, sort of not depending on you, leave the dates a little earlier for "doing some errands." Be busy so that he is jealous of hobbies, work, friends, and wants to win your time. Give the man time to understand how special you are and that he misses.

9. Agree only to what befits you.

It is good to live in peace and harmony, but your opinions do not always have to coincide. You don't have to follow his wishes. Sometimes a minor disagreement can take him by surprise, but it will make him respect you. Remember, a man likes to flirt with a cheerful girl and at the same time communicate with a person who has his own opinion and dignity. Give him the feeling that two persons are harmoniously combined in you: a carefree laugher and a thoughtful intellectual. He will certainly want to figure out how it is possible, and gradually fall in love with both of you!

10. Don't let him know ahead of time that you are in love.

Men are hunters, they are excited by pursuit. In order to fall in love, he will need time, during which interest should not fade away. Do not show your feelings until you understand that he is head over heels in love. Let him know that you like him, that you feel good next to him, but a man should feel that you have not lost your head. The longer the pursuit lasts, the more difficult it will be for him to gain recognition, the more he will appreciate your feelings. One of my clients, who is now successfully married, told me a story. Her chosen one had a bride before their fateful meeting. Everything went to the wedding; he planned to organize a beautiful love confession and marriage proposal in the best traditions of Hollywood melodramas. That is, the girl had a real chance to become a happy wife of a very caring and attentive, successful man. But she confessed her love first. That's it! Nothing. On the same evening, their relationship ended and lost a happy ending. It is still difficult for him to explain what happened then, but his love vanished in a flash. The fact remains - men like to be the first! Do not deprive them of this opportunity, and you will be happy. By the way, the phrase "I love you!" is easy to be replaced by "I'm good with you!" All in all, you really don't have to strain too hard to make a man fall in love with you. Rather, you need to relax and understand: flirting is a game, you should accept some of its conditions, enjoy the process and not depend on the result. Does he have a choice?

SMILE

- Andryusha, why are you angry?

- Because I'm Sasha!

MINUTE OF WISDOM
The angels call it Heaven's desire, the devils call it Hell's own fire, and man, he calls it Love!
Heinrich Heine

Sex on the first date. Pros and cons

At my trainings, girls often ask the question: "On what date can I have sex?". Unambiguously, it should be answered as follows: you can and should have sex, but it is important to follow some rules.

Preferably not on the first date. Only if you both are seized by a sudden unchecked passion, you are not aiming at a serious relationship with this young man and you know that your reputation will not suffer, you can succumb to temptation. But remember: her reputation is important for a woman!

Too frequent change of partners, an abundance of short-term romantic relationships with unfamiliar people lowers self-confidence. I have not met a girl yet who is truly happy with the abundance of sex fast food in her life. Besides, men, in their secret heart, are sure that if you practice sex on the first date, then this is the norm for you, and you behave like this always and with everyone. Agree - this is not a pleasant perception of you. The effect of the first impression has not been canceled. Why then waste your mental strength to prove that you are "not like that"? It's easier just not to create a precedent on the first date.

Have sex just for your own pleasure. Don't use it to capture a man's attention, take a relationship to the next level, or get pregnant in order to make him marry you. Do not be on the bit of his requests just because "it is kind of inconvenient to refuse." Know how to use the best contraceptive - the magic word "no".

Always ask yourself questions: what do you really want, what is behind the desire for intimacy, and how else can you get the same result?

Never have sex because of fear of losing - this is the shortest path to breaking up. Men feel your fears, dependence, their power over you, and their interest in you decrease.

You should have sex if you feel a great desire and it is mutual. When a strong attraction arises and it is no longer possible to restrain sexual energy, it must be used for peaceful purposes. Seduce him! Frankly and brazenly. At least you will get pleasure and, if you are lucky, perhaps the most dizzying sex in your life. And who knows, maybe it will turn out to be unforgettable for your partner too...

It's better later than earlier. You shouldn't count the number of dates after which it is already possible. Men also read women's magazines and know the 10 dating rules (traditional advice from glossy magazines). But it is important to remember that men and women perceive sex differently: we subconsciously perceive it as the beginning of a serious relationship, and they - as the logical end of the courtship period. And if a man did not have time to feel respect for you, fall in love, court, most likely, it will be difficult for you to keep his interest further.

You feel desired. If a man is able to give confidence that you are a special woman in his life, if you understand that he is in love, if next to him your relationship is ripe for bed. But if you have some doubts, trust your intuition. Take time for yourself and him to sort out your feelings.

It is very important how you behave after sex. No need to wait for love confessions and certainty from a man. Turn off the standby mode and switch to other interests. He is active, insists on continuing the relationship - it's great! He does not hurry up to call - don't sit and don't wait for the call! See how he treats you and copy the behavior. You can show a slight disinterest in order to intrigue.

If you think the sex happened too quickly, leave him feeling that it was he who seduced you. Admit your defeat in words: "So I became your next victim. Congratulations, you are a hero! " And disappear - without explanations and calls. Wait for his first step, and then, as if nothing happened, communicate as with an ordinary boyfriend who is seeking your attention.

The main thing is not to strive to consider your future husband in him, while the man looks at you only as a love-mate. *In order not to be disappointed, just do not be fascinated ahead of time.* A person who wants to be close to you is persistent and will not allow you to simply disappear from his life.

When you are wondering whether it is worth having sex with this particular man or not, understand that there are no right or wrong answers, as there is no one ready-made solution for all possible situations.

There is nothing more beautiful in this world than harmonious sexual relations between two people in love. And only you can decide what you want and what you deserve: a passion for one evening or still passionate love.

SMILE

An ingenious sign in one coffee shop: "We don't have Wi-Fi, not because we're miser ... Just communicate with those who you came with!"

LESSON 9

YOU ARE THE BEST! NOT ONE OF THE BEST. ALWAYS REMEMBER ABOUT IT.

Love is an exciting wonderful feeling that is worth experiencing at least once in your life! It is necessary and comes into your life to fill it with new meaning, to give amazing experiences, to make you better, wiser. And in this chapter I will talk about the basic principles of amorousness.

Everything like animals, or the Laws of the jungle and love

You saw Him. Here he is, the man of your dreams! And you already imagine him as a husband with your two little kiddies in his arms. And everything is going so well ... It is a pity that so far only in dreams. Whether you noticed or not, as a rule, your zeal is directly proportional to his lack of desire to court. For some reason, he does not hurry up to become your betrothed.

By the way, it's natural to figure out whether he fits to be your spouse. This is the idea of nature; a woman intuitively immediately selects suitable candidates.

A period of courtship begins; it is the so-called mating game. It will be useful to dig on YouTube and see how this process is carried out by animals. Believe me, in these matters we are not far from the wild. This is where instincts are involved.

It would seem that there is nothing easier: well, an animal feels thanks to the weather-time-climatic conditions that the "hour of love" has struck, that the time has come to procreate offsprings - go forth and multiply ... But no! Each animal tries to show off, to demonstrate itself

141

- something like, this is what I am, choose me. And the female chooses the strongest, the bravest, the most beautiful one. But it does not immediately throw itself into the arms of the winner but arranges its part of the test show: attacks or runs away - in a word, flirts. As a result, these are the best, the winners who multiply. That's how complicated it is! So why should a person have it easier? After all, the pinnacle of creation!..

Nature demands respect for traditions. The natural selection of humans takes place during the courtship period. You seem to be given time to take a closer look, whether your chosen one is so irresistible, in order not to screw things up and put civilization under the threat of extinction. You are being tested for strength.

The law of the jungle is cruel, in which a weak is only prey for a strong. The partner who is more interested in the relationship falls in love first.

The law of the jungle is fair; its basis is "We are of the same blood, you and I." We fall in love, as a rule, with someone with whom we have a lot in common and / or with our ideal "I", with whom we would like to become if we were born men.

Everything in nature is aimed at survival - and it chooses those who are strong in spirit. Even appearance is not primary in matters of survival, other qualities come to the fore - the presence of a character, of an inner core. We instinctively choose those who seem to us in something cooler than ourselves, we are looking for someone better and, when we find, we fall in love without looking back.

The courtship process usually lasts about two months - and here it is important not to give slack, but to play by the rules. There are only three of them: indifference, competition, intrigue. And your behavior should demonstrate all three qualities at the same time because separately they do not work.

INFORMATION FOR REFLECTION

Intrigue (fr. intrigue, from Lat. intrico - "confuse") - interest around an event, phenomenon, or personality due to the uncertainty of the event.

Intrigue can be seen as a way to achieve a goal by manipulating other people.

In addition, the concept of "intrigue" generates the forms "to intrigue", "intriguing", which means "to interest, arouse curiosity" and is obtained mainly as a result of intentional or unintentional omissions, reserves, and ambiguous hints. In small amounts, purposefully intriguing statements can help the cause and not be perceived negatively, but the abuse of this form of speech can be stressful for the interlocutors.

SMILE
- Are you individual?
The crowd all together:
- Yes! We are individual!
A voice from the crowd:
- But not me!

Rule No. 1. "Indifference".

His interest in you should be higher than yours. Politeness and calmness are the best communication tactics during this period. You are not jealous, you are not trying to find out his attitude towards you, you do not control, "you do not call, you do not cry." You have dignity and your own life. You are nice, light, and confident that you are the best choice for any man. Remember: not one of the best representatives of the fair sex, but the best one! And you don't have to be perfect, the main thing is to think that you are perfect. A man must fight for you and your attention. Well, people don't appreciate what comes easily!

Rule No. 2. "Competition".

Confirmation that you are beautiful is crowds of imaginary or real fans (not lovers, but those who dream of catching at least a glance and holding a handle). The task at this stage is to create the feeling that many compete for you. Healthy competition adds excitement to a man and adds points to you. By the way, it's possible to be jealous of hobbies, friends, and interesting life. The main thing is that all this is available, or at least learn to create such an illusion.

Rule No. 3. "Intrigue".

Down with boredom from relationships! Make somebody wait, guess, make assumptions. The task of the intrigue: to focus all the attention of a person on his person, fill his thoughts, and subdue desires. Why do you prefer "some courses" to communicate with him? Where have you been? Where have you mysteriously disappeared?

Why are you "out of sorts"? Why aren't you responding instantly to messages? Why did you cancel the date at the last moment? .. Here is just a small list of questions that are born in his head. Come up with options yourself.

The main principles of intrigue

To make somebody wait.

To make hope.

To make somebody dream.

To arouse curiosity.

To arouse surprise.

To make somebody doubt.

To make somebody guess.

Your behavior in general should demonstrate emotional strength and independence, your calm confidence in yourself, and your own value. You actually try to undermine his self-confidence with your behavior in order to awaken an irresistible desire to prove to you, and to himself, and to Mother Nature that he is the best. These are the "laws of the jungle", the mating games of human civilization.

People fall in love with personalities that are stronger psychologically and emotionally. If you have become a victim of a romantic relationship, it's time to analyze what methods your lover managed to bring you into a state of love. After all, our exes are the best teachers.

Have you sometimes got the feeling that he is less interested in your relationship? That he is the dream of all girls? Did you have a sense of uncertainty? How exactly did he "give" you all these feelings? Remember his behavior, words, and everything that upset you. Having made certain conclusions for yourself, take a few of his tricks into service in order to stop being a victim of circumstances and learn to make others fall in love with you.

Coach exercise "List of zests"

We are all imperfect. Fortunately! After all, perfection is boring! There must be some kind of mystery in a woman, or, in other words, a zest. Imperfections make us more human. You will come across as a super confident person if you learn not only to accept your shortcomings but also to be proud of them. It doesn't matter that, perhaps, you are not enthusiastic about them, the main thing is "...

more cynicism. People like it!" Prepare in advance for attacks on your fragile psyche. Write down a list of your shortcomings - internal and external. Choose 3-4 of the most important ones and figure out how to fend off if they are suddenly noticed. We never talk bad about ourselves - only in a positive way. Make phrases that show you are truly proud of your shortcomings. For example, someone criticizes your weight. Your reaction: "I am proud of my curves. By the way, I am always suspicious of men who throw themselves on the bones. Normal men like soft women!"

My zests	The phrase, showing confidence

Define your personal strategy of seduction

There are no universal tactics to inspire love. In fact, you don't need any advice. You know how to behave correctly. Remember how confident, how perfect you seem to be next to a fan who does not interest you and whose adoration you have no doubt about. This is exactly how you should behave with a man in whom you want to arouse a feeling of love. This is your style of seduction and the right emotional state.

These are your features and the personal secret of female attractiveness. There are several main images of seducers. Think about which one is closer to you.

Freedom-loving. You are a creative, frivolous, enthusiastic, curious, cheerful person, you like to learn new things. Such an image will be ideal for a demonstratively freedom-loving man.

He cannot be kept close by guarantees and recognition requirements. Here you need to act from the opposite, tell him as often as possible: "All people are free. Live for yourself. Do only what you like." Forget about your meetings, make appointments over the phone with "some friends" right in front of him. Never make excuses and openly admire his desire for Freedom! Make him jealous, surprised at your unpredictability. Wake the owner up in him! And he will clasp you by the hand more and more tightly.

Silent. The greater the actor, the longer the pause. Do you like to be silent or you just have nothing to say? Are you by nature not very cheerful or are you just disappointed in something? The main thing is not to complain and not to try to pretend fun that is unusual for you now: people are sensitive to pretense. Feign charming sadness, thoughtfulness, let the pauses be long, and the look mysteriously dreamy. The understatement, neither yes nor no, is a complete mystery. He will have to puzzle why you are silent. Perhaps you are one of those who are not ready to cast pearls before swine. An interest in talking to you appears.

Sudden. Today you are laugher - tomorrow you are as black as thunder. Try to understand why everything has changed so dramatically. The man begins to lose confidence in himself - begins to think that he did something wrong. What has caused this change? And tomorrow you will give him tenderness and adoration. You provoke him into sex, then suddenly you become an ice maiden. The contrast shower invigorates!

Immaculate Angel. It doesn't matter how many men you had before him - you live a dream and continue to believe in the best in man! Yes, only a select few can understand your subtle soul. You are pure and immaculate. Noble and honest, you so sincerely believe in your piety that you easily forget about all your "sins." A man wants to reach for a bright ideal, that is, for you. You consider yourself almost a saint ... He too. A semi-ephemeral creature with a crystal gaze and firm moral principles - a rare man can resist the temptation to seduce such an angel. Oh, how nice it is to constantly feel a halo above your head!

Affectionate kitty. It's natural for you to be gentle. If you were born an animal, you would certainly be a kitten - fluffy, white, playful. You like to cuddle, fondle, smack, sigh languidly, stroke a man by your look, flatter and lisp, goof around, returning him to childhood, where everything was for real. The subject of these emotions feels how you adore him, and it seems to him that no one has ever treated him so tenderly before. And then it turns out that you are affectionate with everyone. But it's late, he has already fallen in love.

Provocateur. Sarcasm is your eternal companion. Plus self-confidence: you will turn any of his questions or statements in your favor. You are skeptical about everything: naivety is not your strong point. Your favorite phrases are: "Oh, all men, when they want to seduce, they say so", "Yeah, otherwise I don't see that you have already fallen in love. Yes, you were just dying of desire, and I could only agree. " From time to time he is ready to kill you, but just not leave.

A girl without fear or reproach. You are self-sufficient and selfish. Your tactic is to attract by repelling. You know how to play on other people's weaknesses and complexes, you show absolutely disinterested behavior, independence from the opinions of others. Being in the company of such a woman, a man feels himself chosen one and begins to be proud of himself. Although, not for long - until the next appraisingly icy look. But after all, you don't send him away - it means ... Well, in general, it means something! Interest is heightened.

Sexy. You are tired of these obsessive men and their attention. Is it really so difficult to notice remarkable intelligence, two higher educations and a gentle soul behind this short leopard skirt, seductive lips and a fourth size breast? "Why are men so primitive? Why are they the same? Do they see only my charms in me? You too, you are looking at me like a cat looks at sour cream, or am I mistaken? " And the man will immediately begin to prove that he is not like the others, looking more closely at you and being seduced. The advertisement is the engine of commerce.

Well, if we talk about what kind of women men like, we can say with confidence - different! And it's great when, in addition to the main image, several more spare ones organically coexist in you; they can be used according to your mood. The main thing is to live and seduce for your own pleasure. Only then the man will be in love and happy next to you.

MINUTE OF WISDOM

Drought. Jews come to the rabbi and ask him to make it rain.

No, the rabbi says to them, - I cannot make this miracle, because you don't have faith in the Lord.

Why do you say that, rabbi?

Because if you really believed, you would come with umbrellas!

SMILE

A girl marries a millionaire. A friend asks her:

- It is probably love at first sight, isn't it?

- At first sight, you would not say that he is a millionaire.

MINUTE OF WISDOM

See how the woman who attracts all the eyes enters the room. How she walks, how she sits down, what gestures she makes in conversation. By classical standards, she can be considered quite ugly, but, despite this, in her figure, her behavior, her gestures there is something that makes up her style and which is very important precisely because all this is not some kind of external decoration, but belongs to her very being.

Coco Chanel

INFORMATION FOR REFLECTION

In 2011, researchers found out that women consider men who look happy less attractive. They prefer guys who come across as either proud and powerful, or gloomy and ashamed. The same concerns confident women. Unfortunately, during the same study, it was found out that proud and self-confident women seem to be less attractive to men.

SMILE

Examples of a woman's reason

- No, I don't mind, just don't agree.

- It's rare that I half-rise from a diet.

- You must finally agree: I'm not stubborn!

- *He is so silent that you want to undress.*
- *I'm in my third marriage. The husband is in the last.*
- *I love to distraction ... to distraction... whom?*
- *He replaced the lenses in my rose-colored glasses.*
- *No, he did not stutter before the wedding.*
- *I will remain faithful to you at interest.*
- *No, you are not just stupid, you are gorgeously stupid.*
- *Years go by, I'm still over thirty.*
- *You can read in his eyes: seven grades.*
- *Hindrances to happiness - you and excess weight.*
- *Here's a scoundrel: blushes - and does not lie!*
- *How timid he is... it's difficult to resist.*
- *Both my mother and the Ministry of Health warned.*
- *He said nothing - and I believed him.*
- *If you loved me like beer!*
- *Handsome as a wolf. But fed by a she-wolf!*
- *Men flock - and past, past ...*
- *He fell asleep without saying goodbye ... I will divorce!*
- *Not to see you. Isn't this happiness?*
- *Covering a decisive "yes" with a timid "no".*
- *He is a bachelor, there are no other merits.*
- *He is a master of love, and a candidate for marriage.*
- *It's time to make peace, tomorrow is payday ...*
- *Tomorrow I will have a hysteric and shopping.*

LESSON 10

FALL IN LOVE WISELY! LOVE TO THE HILT!

Do you want to be loved and you seem to do everything in order to become such, but you are unlucky in love? Are you tired of eternal meetings and partings? It seems that you just keep going around in circles but you really want to be just happy, don't you? What to do? It is possible that you are trying and fidgeting too hard.

Women tend to rush things and fantasize. Both are not beneficial if you are aiming for a long-term relationship. Take a closer look at the candidate, soberly assess his fascination for you. Even if a guy is fully consistent with the idea of an ideal partner, you have no guarantee that he will be instantly fascinated too. Give him time to get to know you. First, you need to understand what love is. The main mistake of all girls is that they do not know how to distinguish between healthy feelings that lead to happy partnerships, and neurotic love, which makes you suffer.

Life is not an audition for a leading role in a Mexican TV series, so stop acting out tragedies, and finally learn to love correctly. And then men who are capable of healthy relationships will be attracted into your life.

About unconditional love

The truest love is unconditional! And this is unconditionally true! As the apogee of the evolution of human emotions, it can really make a person happy. And not just one person, but a whole couple. Only a person is able to love, despite the uselessness of the chosen ones from the point of view of the instincts of survival and reproduction. People love disabled, unattractive, old, sterile, poor - different. That is why we are human, to differ from our furry friends by the greatness of our feelings.

Yes, just to feel unconditional love for an unfamiliar person is at least strange, and sometimes unsafe. Well, it would not occur to you to call the person, who you know a very short time, the best friend, and even trust him with your soul, would it?

In order to become forgiving and unconditional true love takes time, validity check.

Let's get rid of illusions! There is no such thing as genuine, unconditional love between strangers. Love, Friendship, and Trust develop over time and usually involve reciprocity, overcoming, and compassion. And these are conscious decisions, efforts and commitments. The only question is, whether you are ready for it or not. We can talk for a long time about the definition of true love. But brevity is the sister of talent. And you can't say better than it is said in the Bible:

"Love endures for a long time, has mercy, love does not envy, love is not exalted, is not proud, does not rage, does not seek its own, does not get irritated, does not think evil, does not delight in the lie, but delights in the truth, covers everything, believes everything, hopes everything, tolerates everything. Love never stops..."

(Bible; the First Letter of St. Paul to the Corinthians)

Perhaps you are familiar with this thought-worm: "Eh! If only I were wiser, more modest, more tolerant, knew how to forgive!" You begin to punish yourself for the inability to unconditional love and feel ashamed of your ignorance. Thank God, the extra Ferrari is not parked in the garage at the moment, otherwise, you would sell it and zip down to Tibet on emotions. To refine yourself!

And really, where is this fine line between eccentricity, selfishness and justice? Simulating an angel on the earth and trying to be kinder to people, don't we sometimes allow our beloved to shamelessly climb onto our well-groomed heads and wave their legs from there?

We need to understand what we want with this person: love or a love adventure. These are two different strategies. A long-term relationship presupposes an important base - trust, as well as a reasonable approach! But for romantic passion, flirting, trust is not necessary.

In a pleasing long-term relationship, partners experience Love-Acceptance or Love-Affection, which is truly unconditional and resembles in many respects friendship. But for this, a man and a woman must go through such stages: interchange, overcoming, complicity. Then the true meaning will appear in their relationship: just to be together, because it's better with you than without you, and for your sake, I want to become better.

And the relationships *"He doesn't love me, but I love him anyway"*, *"I tolerate for the sake of love"*, *"I suffer, but I hope that he will change soon"* destroy a person's individuality, but don't ennoble him.

Handing the keys to your heart to another, keep the keys to your happiness!

The idea of nature was nevertheless ingenious: love as the crown of the evolution of emotions. Love ennobles, develops, stimulates a person to become better. And this joyful feeling - it is amore naturale! That is, they love you and want to be with you, and it makes you feel good!

Love is incompatible with compulsion. Trying to force to unconditionally accept all the shortcomings of a man, eternal compromises with your own happiness, ignoring your intuition and real needs is the road to suffering. And this is not unconditional love, but an obsession, an addiction that you need to get rid of as soon as possible. These are the consequences of victim psychology.

Feelings are your life energy, and if your beloved man does not replenish it, and you continue to waste it on him, so much the worse for you.

TRUE love is built on trust and exchange.

If you are uncomfortable in a relationship, you do not need to sacrifice yourself and jump into the relationship as if into the deep end, for this abyss will swallow you. Well, if, nevertheless, unrequited love happened to you, find the courage to take responsibility for your feelings and survive this feeling with dignity, developing and improving for yourself, for the sake of your future other, who, perhaps, is waiting for your love and is capable of reciprocity. As Osho said in his book "Love. Freedom. Aloneness": "Love gives you wings to soar high!"

The universal principle of building happy relationships is a strategy of mutual exchange, tit for tat (something like "you - to me, I - to you"), but try to offer a little more than is expected from you. So the partner will sooner have a reciprocal desire to do good things for you.

MINUTE OF WISDOM

There are some flowers of love that bloom only after a longtime closeness. There are also annual flowers: they bloom in the sun for six weeks, but after six weeks they leave forever. There are flowers that need years to bloom, and there are flowers that need many years. The more time it takes, the deeper the love is. But it must be the devotion of one heart to another heart. It must be a silent devotion: eyes to eyes, heart to heart, being to being. This must be understood, not said.

Osho

SMILE

Quarrel in a tightly knit family:
- Go suck a lemon! - Go suck a lemon yourself!
- Let's go together? - Let's go!

Coach exercise "False guilt"

We are often unfair to ourselves. And we also love to torture ourselves with some far-fetched feelings. Although often it is other people who are not entirely right or are simply concerned about their problems. Leave them the right to make their mistakes, and get rid of emotional masochism yourself by answering these simple questions:

What exactly happened?

_____

_____

What were his expectations?

_____

_____

And what is its benefit?

_____

_____

Why do I need it?

_____

_____

What is my specific fault towards this person?

_____

_____

Were there circumstances under which I was forced to act against the interests of another person?

_____

_____

How to understand whether you are in love or not?

Love is a feeling that causes a real storm of chemical, hormonal and emotional surges in our body. You can talk about it endlessly! And, since love gives us one of the deepest experiences, let's figure them out together.

Sense of euphoria

According to Helen Fisher, an anthropologist at Rutgers University, when we fall in love, dopamine level increases in our brain. This pleasure hormone is responsible for desire, motivation, attraction, and addiction. A mass of energy appears, we become excited and full of life. At the same time, you don't need to sleep anymore, sometimes you can even forget about food because all thoughts and desires are concentrated on a loved one. And if you are reciprocated, wings grow behind your back, you feel light and happy! A similar effect is observed in people after using cocaine.

Causeless happiness

Even a call from a loved one evokes such emotions that you are ready to kiss the cat, jump up to the ceiling and hug everything that comes to hand. From the outside, it may seem that you are urgently getting stupid. But the reason is love fever. And you, in general, do not care what others think about it.

Failure to adequately assess the situation and loved one

He seems perfect, the best person on Earth, even his weaknesses are touching! And this is natural, the British scientists came to this conclusion, having examined people looking at photographs of their loved ones on a functional magnetic resonance imaging machine. After all, when we think about the object of desire or see it, such areas of the brain as the temporal, parietal and frontal cortex, which are associated with critical thinking, are deactivated. Perhaps that is why it is difficult for a person in love to objectively assess the subject of emotion.

SMILE

On a dating website:

- My name is Lena, I have graduated from Cambridge, recently returned home, my dad is a prominent banker. And you?

- My name is Eduard, I have two steel plants in the Urals and a network of gas stations. Lena, let's go to a restaurant in the evening?

- With pleasure! Which one?

- I really love oriental cuisine, and you?

- Well ... I don't mind.

- Then at seven in the evening in "Uchkuduk"?

- And what minibus goes there?

- No. 36 and No. 47. But you will have to wait for No. 47 a long time.

- And it's difficult to catch No. 36 at our bus stop. I'd better take a tram.

- Ok. I'll be waiting!

You can't think of anyone else

When you are emotional, you cannot think of anything or anyone else. Thoughts about your beloved are constantly swarming in your head, which makes it simply impossible to work, to focus on other interests, on that which does not refer to your feelings. This is due to norepinephrine, a chemical entity that is released along with dopamine in the brain when you fall in love.

Sexual desire

You want him all the time, you feel a strong physical attraction only to him - other men cease to exist for you as objects of desire.

Butterflies in the stomach

Often people describe such emotions as follows: "It seems that butterflies tickle your belly from the inside with their wings." The sensation of butterflies in the stomach is especially vivid when you love at first sight. You're nervous and that's okay. Some scientists believe that this is due to the release of adrenaline in the body.

You easily get depressed and euphoric over trifles

When we are in love, the level of serotonin in the brain reaches its peaks in positive and negative values. It can raise to the peak of happiness and lower into the abyss of despair. The trigger for changing the emotional background can be such little things that you would not even pay attention to in a normal state. It is clear that it is rather difficult to be for a long time in such a state, the symptoms of which are very similar to a mental disorder, so nature took care of us. According to the previously mentioned Helen Fisher, amorousness can last no longer than two years, or a little more if you have to hide it.

And what's next? Does undying love exist? Don't worry, it exists! But whether amorousness will grow into real affection forever or not depends only on you and your partner. And this is a completely different story ...

SMILE

A blonde comes to the casino, goes to the roulette wheel, bets on 22 and wins. She bets again and wins again. She bets once again, and she wins again. She is asked:

- How did you do it?

- I came here on the 7th train. At the hotel, I was put in room number 7. And the hotel is located on the street at number 7.

- So, what does 22 have to do with it?

- How? Isn't 7 + 7 + 7 equal to 22?

How to distinguish true love from neurosis?

Dependence and codependency this is how psychotherapists call neurotic's Love. The neurotic girl herself considers her love to be great and unique, and the greater the love, the more suffering it causes.

She waits for it all her life. In general, the life of any neurotic is full of expectations ... Now a neurotic woman waits that "love will come unwittingly when you don't expect it at all." Then she waits for courtship and gifts, a marriage proposal and half a kingdom into the bargain. Then - a gorgeous wedding and honeymoon in the Bahamas. And later she assumes that she will be loved and cherished until the end of her days. At the same time, the girl needs precise guarantees that everything will happen exactly according to her plan, as in the picture from her visualization. Healthy and beautiful love does not really expect anything: it just gives, because only by giving you can obtain. The love of an adult needs no guarantees.

It is the ability of a person to live in a state of uncertainty that distinguishes a healthy person from an immature, infantile person. As the American psychologist Karen Horney well said in this regard: "The difference between love and a neurotic need for it is that the main thing in love is the very feeling of affection. Whereas the primary feeling of a neurotic is the need to gain confidence and calmness." Therefore, only clear deadlines, obligations and fulfillment of often overstated requirements make it possible for a neurotic to finally relax and stop worrying. A person with an adequate attitude does not need guarantees: he knows that life can make adjustments to any plans, and is ready for this.

The neurotic woman does not love herself and considers herself unworthy of love in the depths of her soul. This is expressed in ostentatious external self-confidence and a thirst for attention to her person. Sometimes she takes ordinary signs of attention and politeness too seriously and falls in love as if in return. Her love is a reaction of gratitude for the kindness shown to her. This type of person is in acute need of attention and care: in childhood, they were not loved enough, society underestimated them, they did not realize themselves as specialists - therefore, they need, like air, at least someone to hug and fondle them. They are so hungry that they are ready to feed on any handouts of attention.

The neurotic woman is jealous. Her attitude towards herself is constantly fluctuating: now she is a goddess, then she is complete insignificance. Because of this, she constantly doubts that someone, potentially, is able to fall in love with her real, and carefully monitors that the beloved person does not distribute a crumb of attention on the side.

The neurotic woman is very suspicious. She always fancies something: sometimes that nobody loves her, sometimes that she is not loved enough; sometimes that nobody appreciates her, sometimes that she is underestimated. Confidence in her partner's feelings can only be caused by a romantic act, and it does not last long - as long as the victim of love remains impressed by the event.

The neurotic woman waits all the time. Quarrels, resentments, demonstrative walk-offs, or playing the silent game - she accumulates "material" and endures to the last. What for? After all, if you had said everything on time and calmly, you wouldn't have to swear later.

Neurotic love cannot make any part truly happy. In fact, neurosis is a hypersensitivity to negative emotions. When the defense mechanisms of the psyche are already so weakened, they cannot cope with daily stress.

It seems that the girl is trying to be the best for the chosen one, to bring him joy, sincerely wants her partner to be fun and good with her. But she just can't do it for free, only in exchange for something: text messages, romantic dinners, fidelity, and the like - the list never ends, because a neurotic woman is insatiable in love because it is impossible to saturate internal problems with external solutions. And, oh, woe is you, beloved! If you do not live up to expectations (tired, or misinterpreted vague hints, or do not have telepathic abilities) - that's it, it's the end of the world! She goes offended. Resentment and guilt are two childish and not very effective strategies in the long run, but the only available reactions for a neurotic.

To arouse compassion, accuse, take offense, blackmail, humiliate - in this she has no equal, she is a virtuoso manipulator. Often, in order to be loved, a neurotic woman specially studies the techniques of NLP and generally tries very hard to be loved, not ignored, completely unconcerned about how a man feels in such a relationship.

In order to check whether you are in love or is it an ordinary neurosis, just ask yourself the question: "If now a fan who is more beautiful, more generous, more attentive appeared in your life, would you leave the thoughts about your today's beloved?" It is a pity that almost 100% of love sufferers answer, almost without thinking: "Yes!" But just a minute ago they were ready to give their lives for their beloved. However, in only a token way ... And that life, which they do not value themselves. Otherwise, only bright feelings would be allowed into it, they would fill it with friends, extraordinary work, exciting hobbies, interesting books, beautiful music. Then there would be absolutely no time or desire to suffer. There would be so much energy and harmony that they would like to share it. And the girl would feel how beautiful and inspiring relationships can be when people try to give each other joy without expecting anything in return.

MINUTE OF WISDOM
I see what is good, I praise it, but I am attracted to another.

Ovid

MINUTE OF WISDOM
Love is an active interest in the life and development of what we love. Where there is no active interest, there is no love.
Erich Fromm, German psychologist

SMILE
- *What is female bitchiness?*
- *This is an attempt to transform a man into a hybrid of a vibrator and an ATM.*
Narcissists. How are cold seducers attractive and dangerous?

Marketers around the world, carefully choosing expressions and pictures, construct in our heads an Eden of luxury and pleasure, which you will surely get into if you are not like everyone else!

It is not fashionable to be ordinary, SUCCESS accompanies exceptional people! All glossy magazines are dedicated to the special, unique and inimitable. They get everything excellent: the best girls, the best cars and the best resorts ...

Narcissists are prominent representatives of modern culture. Of course, every person is unique. Each of us has an inherent ambition, purposefulness, ability to charm. We all try to please and get what we want. Only sometimes it begins to take hypertrophied forms, where there is no longer a sense of the naturalness of relationships and the importance of other people and their needs.

Narcissists are charismatic and unmatched, and it's easy to fall into their charms. But who you should definitely not fall in love with is them. This love will always be unrequited.

In love, they are sophisticated and the most dangerous seducers. Oh! You have never been so happy! You have never been so desired! Nobody has been so romantic before! Your life has never looked like a fairy tale yet! That's it! There was nothing real there! The only thing that doesn't go according to the magic scenario is the lack of an inspiring happy ending. Relationships with narcissists are always toxic, disappointments are inevitable, and the end is predictable ...

INFORMATION FOR REFLECTION

All our subconscious desires, contradictory in nature and unlimited in content, wait for their fulfillment in love. Our partner must be strong and at the same time helpless, ascetic and sensual, lead and agree to the role of the follower at the same time. He must rape us and remain gentle, devote his time only to us, and intensely engage in creative work.

As long as we sincerely believe that he can really accomplish all of this, he is surrounded by a halo of sexual overestimation. We take the power of this overestimation for the power of our love, but in reality, we are only demonstrating the intensity of our desires, because the very nature of these requirements makes them unfulfillable.

Karen Horney, American psychologist

Why does he need you?

"Illusion is needed to hide the emptiness inside," said one of the classics of psychoanalysis. And the narcissist is a master of innuendo, he deceives himself and you. Sometimes reluctantly, it is an innate talent, so to say.

Fabulous courtship, beautiful gestures, and he himself is like a picture - so successful and exceptional. Feeling of the theatricalism. It is impossible to feel real human closeness with them and they are not ready to take responsibility for another. You are an emotional resource for them. For all the external self-sufficiency, they have a gaping emptiness of real emotions inside them.

How to pin down Narcissus?

HE IS FASCINATING! Wherever you look - there are only medals everywhere. Handsome, successful, sporty! You are astonished! There is one "but" - he is personally never satisfied with his results (there is no guarantee that he will ever admit it even to himself). And he is sincere because the inner emptiness cannot be filled with any external achievements.

YOU ARE ALONE NEXT TO HIM! Even when he tries to do the impossible for you, is generous and attentive, and surrounds with dizzying flips of courtship, you do not feel sincerity and warmth in the relationship. It is impossible to give away what you do not have yourself.

YO-YO-EFFECT. Idealization and devaluation is a common story in the development of a relationship with a narcissist. At first, it seems that He is ready to do anything for you! He charms, tries ... He exalts you to the skies, then disappears. And so over and over again.

HE IS GREEDY FOR PRAISE. For its sake, in fact, he lives and absolutely does not accept criticism. He believes that he is surrounded by envious people and losers, among whom he numbers everyone who does not deify him. Usually, he is intolerant of people's shortcomings.

GUILT! You constantly feel guilty towards him. He masterfully inspires it and then pulls the strings so that you appease him and beg for forgiveness, and in order to feel control and power over your emotional world again.

NO STABILITY. With all his resources and the kind of actions performed for you (read "for the sake of recognition"), fantasies about the future, assurances of eternal love and fidelity, you feel constantly in limbo.

NARCISSUS IS A DIFFICULT PERSONALITY. Although you constantly unravel his behavior and try to correct your mistakes, you cannot understand him in any way. If you feel better, I can say that he does not understand himself. On the one hand, he needs people around him, on the other, he avoids any real intimacy. He is able to talk for hours about the mystery of his nature, involving you in philosophical discussions about his person.

When will awareness come?

It is almost impossible to leave a narcissist, he is too good. It is usually he who cools down. Western psychologists have noticed that in a normal happy relationship, a period of stable, calm confidence in a partner occurs after about 4 months - for narcissists, this is a period of withdrawal, it is usually the most difficult and dramatic for a partner.

What to do?

There is one correct answer in this puzzle - to stop solving it and run quickly and as far as possible, saving your self-respect and the remnants of mental harmony.

The narcissist does not understand the word "give", he will only "take", "use" and consider his love for you as the greatest indulgence. The more you try, the less interesting you seem to him. You must be the princess of Monaco, and then, perhaps, the qualitative indicators of his victory will exceed the quantitative ones. And he will stop - vanity will prevail. But usually, the narcissist is in constant search of the Ideal Woman (a reason that sounds good) and longs for new victories that will amuse his ego (the real reason). This is Man - a holiday that cannot last forever.

Exceptional men, or "Mr. Right", who must be excluded from the candidates for admirers

Agree, if you ended the relationship with the wrong candidates at the very beginning of the relationship - how many disappointments you could have avoided. After all, we often enter into relationships because of boredom, "for health" or, thinking that love comes with a habit, even when we see that the guy clearly does not correspond to our girlish dreams. Stop! Don't waste your time, it's too valuable resource, especially for a girl. Let the "exemplar" go free - not your size.

Usually, three meetings are enough to understand this. Ask him questions about dreams, problems, and listen, be attentive.

We often think that for the sake of love a man can change or that we will get used to it, and everything is under control ... But you are an adult girl and you understand that time is working against you. Women are emotional: we get used to and fall in love often contrary to common sense and our plans, forgetting that a man can be remade only in small things, but not his character and view of life.

Save your precious time and resources
And while you haven't committed folies yet, I would like to introduce you into the types of men from whom you need to run away immediately and without a backward glance.

1. Drinkers and / or drug addicts.
No comments! Pay special attention to the relatives of the chosen one, alcoholism is often inherited.

2. Emotionally cold men. If he has never experienced warm feelings before, even for his homeland, do not try to melt the ice in the heart of this Snow Queen in the shape of a man. A person either has the ability to love or does not have it. And besides, a man who is not able to share emotions with you is often stingy in other areas of life. Do you need it?

3. Men who were brought up in a very patriarchal family where a woman is man's friend. Sometimes you look at such people and think: "It would be better if your name was Mowgli and you were raised by monkeys." If you are looking for a husband-partner, a husband-friend, be careful with this type - before the wedding he will be nice, but as soon as Mendelssohn's waltz sounds, the model of his family's behavior will turn on.

4. Men who talk badly about their former passions. Especially if he always met unhinged, crazy women. Madmen are in madhouses - I hope he did not meet her there. And in order to imagine what his ex was, look in the mirror. She is a woman like you. She also had plans, dreams of happiness together. Think about what his features made her lose control. Maybe he's just not ready for an honest, serious relationship and avoids responsibility?

5. Men who are too busy: to help, to call back on time, to meet when you want it. As in the song of the music band "Chaif": "If I did not come, then what the hell do you need me for?"

6. Too married men who are not appreciated or loved by their wives. So there is a reason for this. Otherwise, he would not be with you now, but next to his beloved, to avoid a new reason for dislike. Even if he divorces over time (by the way, there is no guarantee, but your precious time will be lost), where is the guarantee that the same will not be told about you to a new mistress?

7. Pessimists. Everything is bad for them ... It won't be better! The more likely is that you will be infected with this gloomy outlook on life but not he will begin to relate to the world and at the same time to your relationship with joy.

8. Men with whom you have different life values. It is very serious. For example, you like luxury hotels or a savage vacation, a certain style of dress, makeup, your girlfriends - it's all your choice! And if it goes against his ideas about correctness and life values, such a marriage is fragile. If you have to constantly make excuses, then you don't need to make excuses, you need to run away. From him - to a bright future, where you will meet a guy who will admire even your weaknesses.

9. Men with whom you are more often bad than good. I repeat - it won't be better!

10. A man who needs to be saved - financially or morally. It will feed on your resources and, like a butterfly, will fly with renewed vigor to the next dandelion - to collect pollen of woman's nobility.

A real man can handle everything himself. The only thing he needs is your belief in him and your love.

I did not talk about fighters, pathologic meanies, gigolos and deviant members of the population, because I want to believe that you will not develop relationships with such types.

In general, when you next meet "Mr. Right" with the above mentioned qualities or a bouquet of them, even if he has a "Bentley" in the role of a white horse, let him gallop by!

The main thing is to remember that for a ***woman her man is her destiny!***

Choose using common sense, and then fall in love to the hilt!

SMILE

Online Dating:

- Let's meet at nine in the evening near the subway. How will I recognize you?

- I'm wonderful ...

How to avoid becoming a victim of a manipulator-storyteller?

Recently, by leaps and bounds, the number of pickup courses has been growing, at the end of which each graduate has a golden key to the hearts of naive girls.

Of course, a lot depends on the decency of the guy, but on the same courses, they teach not to pay extra attention to such outdated concepts. "From quantity to quality!", "Seduce more girls in order to find one and only one!" - sometimes even the most humane teachers present information under such a sauce. The fact remains, and in order not to be quantitative material for seduction skills training, you need to learn to recognize and resist the psychic attacks of novice or experienced macho.

Manipulation is the psychological influence of another person, aimed at making you do what he needs, and according to your own will. The manipulator's task is to subjugate your will, make you a potential victim, a puppet, a psychological masochist. This is a way to lead you into a jungle of guesswork, illusion and vain hopes, a way to steal your life energy.

Of course, love is not a permanent, one hundred percent feeling of eternal grace. There are ups and downs, there are different moods, but only with a manipulator you feel a suffocating dependence on his mood, constantly experience mental discomfort, balance on the verge of love and hatred for your tormentor. It seems to you that if you tolerate a little and do not take offense or somehow change, improve, then everything will work out by itself. But here is my advice to you: it is better to immediately abandon the manipulator guy if you are not sure that you are by nature a predator or are able to withstand permanent psychic attacks and at the same time maintain complete mental harmony.

In relationships, you should trust your feelings and remember the rule: **if something seems to you, it doesn't seem**. Stop and analyze your feelings. How often do you have a feeling of spiritual chaos in this relationship? Ask yourself: "Do I feel good with him?", "What do I really want?", "What do I get?", "How can I change the situation?" And start acting. As soon as you take the first step, your attention will immediately switch from the problem to finding optimal solutions.

Also remember that a woman should be emotionally stronger than a man, calmer, which means that your mood should not be tied to thoughts about him. It is important not to lose yourself, your little joys, friends, hobbies, dreams, the ability to enjoy life next to a young man. It is important not to become a victim of love.

Any experienced manipulator starts by trying to evoke feelings in you, so that later he could easily play them. First, he immerses you in a fairy tale, where he is a prince, showering you with compliments, flattery, flowers, calls, caring text messages. He is so helpful and gentle that it seems to you that he is completely in captivity of your charm and with him, it is really possible to build that very cloudless future that he sometimes hints at. You relax, you start to trust the person, he becomes your idol, but ... it's too early! After all, this is just an embellishment. As affection develops on your part, his desire to be next to you more often disappears, and here real games for adults begin. He dictates the terms with his behavior and words, and you do your best to please in order to return his previous favour. He just held the time to bind you and get to know you better, so to speak, to investigate, because he was used to acting for sure, not wasting energy on unnecessary gestures. Now he knows about your weaknesses, fears and dreams. He will skillfully manipulate your complexes, pressing them at the right moment, like buttons.

Does he know that you're jealous? Trust me, he'll find a way to make you worry more. Hints about the flawless appearance or character of his exes, constant checking of messages on the phone and mail in your presence, attention to pretty girls, compliments to your friends, and much more will keep your possessive instinct awake. Remember: **while you are jealous, you are in his power,** and manipulation is a struggle for power in a relationship.

Do you seem fat or ugly to yourself? He will kindly take the menu when you try to order dessert, examining your figure with reproach. Are you conscientious? He will try to constantly appeal to pity and righteousness. **Your weaknesses are the source of the manipulator's strength, he will use your fear to lose him, and you will become a subordinate.**

Have you told him about your dreams? Now he just needs to give you the hope that he is able to help you to make them come true, and you will enthusiastically follow in the direction indicated by him to the magic sounds of the "pipe" of his promises and his expectations.

How can you avoid becoming a victim? You have to be vigilant. For this, I will talk about the main types of manipulations. As it is said: forewarned means forearmed!

"Sweet-voiced siren". He showers you with compliments, like petals of invisible roses ... You relax ... And you feel like a wonderful person, capable of beautiful deeds for the sake of your beloved. Remember, man is not words, **man is deeds. And judge him by real deeds and not beautiful speeches.**

"Victim of Love". He is so unhappy, and your predecessors were so unfair to him, that it is very difficult for him to believe in love again. He appeals to your pity. These are starving children of Africa and homeless kittens that need to be saved and spared, and an adult man must understand himself before starting a new relationship. All these stories are aimed at moving you to pity and making you invest more in relationships, without expecting anything in return - what can you take from the poor?

"Demonstration of doubt." He shares his fears that he does not deserve you, admits that he is too selfish, talks about his shortcomings

and is very, very worried that this may interfere with your eternal love. And you start to calm him down and say that this is not so, that he is wonderful and everything will be fine - thereby convincing yourself of this. Well, that was his real goal, and you did his job for him. Excellent!

A subspecies of this manipulation is his questions like "Why did you fall in love with me?" or "Why do you love me so much? I do not understand…"

I described the expected reaction above.

"Let's live here and now", "Life is short", "Who knows what awaits us tomorrow? Let's enjoy the moment! " - this is an approximate text and the meaning of one more manipulation and at the same time his way to avoid responsibility in a relationship.

"The guy in great demand". He managed to convince you that you have many competitors. Now you try your best not to miss him and enter the fight for the male. You worry, you try to be the kindest, most forgiving, most undemanding … And at this time he enjoys this zeal and his ability to turn you around his finger.

"Soul striptease". His thoughtful frankness provokes your stories about the time when you were in love or experienced great emotions. The main thing for him is to unleash your feelings, and then the usual projection will work. That is why so often clients fall in love with psychotherapists - emotions bring them closer.

"Gentle touches". He speaks little and promises little, but he is so gentle. He holds your hand, looks into your eyes, strokes gently. Although, from time to time he suddenly withdraws or forbids touching him. But these are details. It is important that he gives what you need - the warmth of human relations (instead of real actions!). And you're so afraid of losing it!

"Immersion in a fairy tale". He dreams out loud about what a delightful life awaits him, and you are already drawing pictures in your mind and desperately begin to want to become a part of it. To warm-up, he may even ask provocative questions like "Would you like this

kind of life?" And you want to shout: "Yes!" But with annoyance, you realize that in fact, no one offered you anything. This is a common curiosity to spark your imagination.

"Waiting for a miracle." He constantly makes you wait - phone calls, dates, his decisions. He plays with you: "stretching in time" is a classic of manipulation.

"Disappearance". A favorite trick is to disappear under the pretext of having to sort out his feelings or being busy at work, etc. Sometimes without notification, often for an indefinite period. This is done so that you have time to get exhausted and appreciate his super significance for you.

"Holier-than-thou". He seems like a harmless boy. And you are constantly ashamed of yourself - either for commercialism (you want flowers, restaurants, gifts, and this is not the main thing in a relationship, he reasons), then for your sexuality, then for impatience, then for your stupidity. And you try to correspond as much as possible to the righteous principles that are simply beneficial for him to preach.

"Finger-pointing". He is never guilty, only circumstances or other people prevent him from being with you, or loving you with all his heart, or keeping a promise ... And you believe, of course!

"Delay in time". He is ready for anything, though not today ... When? Someday. And he did not refuse, but he did nothing. An unoriginal, but very effective method of manipulation. And you calmed down, and you will wait and again concentrate your thoughts on the future, embedding his persona in your rainbow plans.

"Contrast shower". Today he is an amorousness itself, and tomorrow he is a super-withdrawn personality. Now he is gentle, then - aloof, throwing text messages today, and disappearing tomorrow. Playing on the senses is like a roller coaster. Emotions are exacerbated, and you try to find an explanation for his behavior, blame yourself,

look for flaws in yourself and worry. And you mentally over-focus on this relationship.

The Manipulator is an energy vampire. He needs your tension, attention, emotional stress, concentration on him - so he is saturated with psychic energy. He constantly needs to feed a sense of his own worth. In fact, he is an unhappy person who needs love himself but does not know how to get it. However, you should not feel sorry for him - he will definitely use your compassion for his own purposes. You shouldn't be offended, because you can only blame yourself. Although he uses a remarkable innate or acquired talent for controlling someone else's consciousness, the choice of reaction is always yours. Next to such a guy, you need to learn how to manage feelings, become emotionally independent from him, or look for a simpler, homely guy.

The best tactic in dealing with a manipulator is to make friends with him, accept him as he is, become indulgent, not make any long-term plans. Or become his "mirror" - to behave the way he does: to play the same games and according to the same rules. At the same time, it is important to maintain a state of inner comfort. Become brave, not dwell on your own torment, stop trying to meet other people's expectations, deal with feelings and desires and, being on his wave, using his own methods, do what you need and follow your own plans.

SMILE

Sometimes you remember your exes and involuntarily begin to doubt your adequacy.

MINUTE OF WISDOM

An arrow fired by you to another will fly around the globe and pierce your back.

Eastern wisdom

INFORMATION FOR REFLECTION

Nancy McWilliams - a classic of modern psychoanalysis, the author of a textbook on psychoanalytic diagnostics, distinguishes among other criteria for determining a person's mental well-being the ability to love as the ability to get involved in relationships, to open up to another person. To love him such as he is: with all the strengths and weaknesses. Without idealization and depreciation. It is the ability to give, not to take. This also applies to parental love for children, and partner love between a man and a woman.

MINUTE OF WISDOM

A woman in love with you can inspire you to heights that you never dreamed of. And she asks nothing in return. She just needs love. And this is her natural right.

Osho

MINUTE OF WISDOM

Anyone who wishes to profess good in all cases of life will inevitably die, faced with many people alien to good.

Nicolo Machiavelli, Italian thinker, philosopher, writer

You have to play noughts and crosses with a man. If you are noughts for him, you need to cross out him.

Marilyn Monroe

SMILE

Girls, watch football! It will teach you at least two useful actions - to score and to kick-off ...

The art of truly loving

In order to understand what true love is, you need to be able to experience it yourself. It's possible to talk about love for a long time. It can be poetry, it can be music, it can be in different languages. You can use scientific terms or corny novels, or you can talk about it with your friend at tea, or with a loved one in the heat of passion.

Where does it come from? Where does it go? And why does it scratch the soul when leaving,?

It is an endless theme that excites souls in their attempts to find the truth. But I have never met a better understanding of love than that of Erich Fromm. And it is not necessary to read the whole works to understand the important things. After all, it happens that sometimes a phrase heard and understood in time changes one's fate.

I want you to read carefully each of the quotes, especially the first one, it is my favorite quote.

- If I love, I take care, that is, I actively participate in the development and happiness of another person, I am not a spectator.

- If children's love comes from the principle: "I love because I am loved", then mature love comes from the principle: "I am loved because

I love." Immature love screams, "I love you because I need you!" Mature love thinks, "I need you because I love you."

- Selfless obsession with each other is not proof of the power of love, but only evidence of the immensity of the loneliness that preceded it.

- If a person experiences love according to the principle of possession, it means that he seeks to deprive the object of his "love" of freedom and to keep him under control. Such love does not bestow life, but suppresses, destroys, strangles, kills it.

- Most people believe that love depends on the object, and not on their own ability to love. They are even convinced that since they do not love anyone other than the "beloved" person, this proves the power of their love. This is where the delusion manifests itself - the object-orientation. This is similar to the state of a person who wants to paint, but instead of learning to paint, he insists that he just has to find a decent model: when this happens, he will paint perfectly, and it will happen by itself. But if I really love some person, I love all people, I love the world, I love my life. If I can say to someone "I love you", I should be able to say "I love everything in you", "I love the whole world thanks to you, I love myself in you".

- If a person is able to fully love, then he loves himself as well; if he is able to love only others, he cannot love at all.

It is generally accepted that amorousness is already the top of love, while in fact, it is the beginning and only the possibility of finding love. It is generally accepted that this is the result of the mysterious attraction of two people to each other, an event that occurs by itself. Yes, loneliness and sexual desires make falling in love easy, and there is nothing mysterious about it, but this is the success that goes away as quickly as it came. People do not become loved by chance; your own ability to love causes love in the same way that interest makes a person interesting.

- You must find yourself in your loved one, and not lose yourself in him.

MINUTE OF WISDOM

A compliment must be more truthful than the truth.
Hugo Steinhaus, philosopher

Coach exercise "Love is ..."

Remember the men who loved you and whom you loved.
Continue phrases.
"I know that I love when ..."

_____

_____

_____

"I know that I am loved when ..."

_____

_____

_____

"Love for me is ... "

_____

_____

_____

MINUTE OF WISDOM
Ten important quotations about LOVE
A love that has survived a breakup is rewarded with eternity.

Elchin Safarli

If you meet your true love, it won't go anywhere from you - not in a week, not in a month, not in a year.

Gabriel García Márquez

You do not love the one with whom you go to bed, but the one next to whom you wake up.

Theodore Van Gehren, collector,
founder of the Erotic Museum in Amsterdam

Love is the only thing that makes a person stronger, a woman more beautiful, a man kinder, a lighter soul, and life more beautiful!

Friedrich Nietzsche

Having found love within yourself, you will find it everywhere!
Amu Mom, author of spiritual practices

The attraction of the souls turns into friendship, the attraction of the mind turns into respect, the attraction of bodies turns into passion. And only all together can turn into love.
Confucius

You should know that freedom is the highest value, and if love does not give you freedom, then it is not love.
Osho, Indian spiritual leader

Don't beg for love, hopelessly loving
Do not wander under the window of the unfaithful, grieving.
Like beggar dervishes, be independent -
Maybe then they will love you.
Omar Khayyam

Three things make a person happy: love, interesting work, and the opportunity to travel.
Ivan Bunin

Love is like a tree: it grows by itself, roots itself deeply in our being, and continues to flourish over a heart in ruin.
Victor Hugo

Love runs away from those chasing it, and those who run away it throws itself on their necks.
William Shakespeare

LESSON 11

Play by your own rules!

Manage the situation, otherwise, the situation will begin to manage you

A woman who knows how to play a beautiful and pleasant game, in the end, always achieves what she wants. It is worth studying the basic rules of relationships in order to add a personal charm to them and remake them for yourself.

We respect people who are principled, have dignity, charisma, and a clear position. Be like that! Become wiser. It is easy to do this if you carefully analyze your experience and benefit from it - new rules of behavior and thinking. This is the only way to get a new result.

Create your own philosophy! The experience of the past must be accepted through awareness and learning from it, rather than mourning it over and over again. The only way to change your life for the better and correct the mistakes of the past is to change your views one day. Create your own personal philosophy of life.

These are your effective rules of life, the sum of everything you know and value. These rules will bring you closer to the life you dream about.

Take failures and mischance as life experiences! The universe never sends us trials that we are unable to overcome. Instead of "WHY is this happening to me?" ask yourself the question: "WHY am I given this situation? What important can this teach me? "

It makes no sense to constantly look back at the past and regret missed opportunities, clearing the debris of memories. You have "today and now" to focus your energy on what you really want.

Conclusions. Awareness. Solutions. Make your life conscious, ask yourself questions after significant and emotional events, impressions and knowledge received: "What have I realized more clearly? What conclusions have I made? What decision am I making? "

People don't fall in love because of gratitude or pity. People fall in love with a person's individuality! People love self-confident one!

This is how people are arranged - they do not appreciate what comes easily to them. The more you try to please everyone (and then yourself), the less valuable you will feel. From my professional experience, I can judge that this is the fate of the girls who are deeply insecure.

The best way out is to start behaving like a confident girl, and, as psychologists promise, very soon your inner world will also be rebuilt to a new behavioral model. An English proverb says, "Fake it till you make it". So JUST DO IT!

There is a time for everything. Basic Rules of relations development

Essentially, love between a man and a woman can be classified as love-friendship, love-romance, and love-attachment. One of the main delusions of beautiful princesses is the expectation of unearthly, vehement love, imposed by actions about supermen and slush melodrama. But let's not confuse cinematography and real life. The task of the film industry is to evoke a storm of emotions in you in just two hours. And I must say, some films do a good job with this. So, romantic love is chosen for spectacularity. And often in its most intense form - love-mania. Such addiction-love also has a right to exist - it is not bad sometimes to lose your appetite and sleep, to live a dream. But there is time for everything.

Women tend to express their emotions more strongly than men, and often too prematurely. The correct attitude to your personal life is based on an understanding of the simple laws of human communication. For clarity, I have developed a pyramid of relationships.

It is based on the first category of men - "Admirer". It can be numerous. They are actually your friends, only in male appearance. To rise to the next step of the pyramid, in the "Lovers" category, a man must make gestures for you, otherwise, he will never appreciate you. Man is not words, man is deeds! Therefore, the most successful and worthy man gets to the top of the pyramid, in the category "Husband".

Remember: in order not to be disappointed, you must not be fascinated ... beforehand! And don't take a man seriously until he has proven the seriousness of his intentions! *In a relationship, it is important for a woman to turn off the sound and look at the man's actions.*

And here is the pyramid itself.

Husband
Lover
Admirer

"Admirer" category

This is love-play, love-communication, love-interest. Men in this category are your fan club. These are your "friends", and you shouldn't limit their number.

A woman should have a choice! Sexual interest has arisen, but there is still no depth, no mutual obligations, it is naive to wait for loyalty and expensive gifts at this stage. It should be just interesting and pleasant for you to communicate with each other. Show emotional generosity towards the candidate, tame him, give him a basic sense of security, reliability. Agree with him in a conversation, look for something in common and note it, always be glad to call. I will repeat the postulate from lesson number 5: the more often and more time we spend with a potential partner, the more interesting we become for him, the more he starts to like us. Therefore, at the very beginning of a relationship, a woman needs to look for various reasons, if a man does not do this, in order to spend as much time with him as possible. But at the second stage of the relationship, when it seems to you that you have already spent enough time with each other, when he has already got used to you, change your tactics so that the hunter's instinct awakens in him. But for now, tame him. We are all full of doubts, and so that they do not win at this stage, and the communication does not end, let him understand that he can count on something more. A man should feel it, not get it!

The task of this stage of the relationship is to collect the maximum information about a person, establish good contact, communication, and lay a solid foundation for relationships.

Create "empathy" - this is a psychology term for psychological comfort. The result: a feeling of sympathy and mutual confidence. Not yet faith, but confidence. The motivation for men at this stage: a thirst for adventure and sex; for women: a desire for communication and romance. These are the mechanisms that make us move up the pyramid.

"Lover" category

This is love-fancy, love-eros, love-passion. Before a man is here, you must give him the feeling of the Game, where you are the Main Prize! (With all the ensuing consequences!) This is a period of motives deepening - a man must internally decide why, apart from sex, he needs you, so that he has a desire to stay with you and move up the pyramid to the "Husband" category. Become a part of his interests, his company, his life. This is where instincts come into play. He has to make sure that you are the best and it is not easy to get you. You need to become mysterious and save your openness and simplicity for the family. A more detailed description of the strategy of behavior at this stage was offered in lesson number 10. Giving and receiving pleasure, suffering and singing serenades, committing reckless acts are the signs of this stage. This is the stage of falling in love, and it usually lasts no more than two years. It will be great if, in the process of your passionate relationship, you feel confident in him, his feelings, and your relationship will move on to the next stage.

It is believed that if a man did not make an offer of marriage at this stage and/or did not take responsibility and care for the woman on himself, then he will never do it. I largely agree with this statement.

"Husband" category

It is love-responsibility, love-decision, love-exchange. The most worthy one gets to "the top". Someone who has earned your trust and respect. I am absolutely sure that you need to marry a man who, in addition to passion, evokes in you deep respect for his person. After all, if we despise a person even a little, then long-term and happy relations with him cannot be built. Despisal, like disgust, is a cumulative feeling and does not disappear over time. A woman, as a rule, wants to create a family because of the desire for a sense of security in this world, a "reliable man's shoulder" (it happens at the level of instincts, you cannot argue against nature) and warm, trusting, human relations (care, attention, psychological and moral support). A man chooses a Woman to be his wife as a worthy trophy, which he won and is proud of it, and because of the desire to bring coziness and comfort into his life and home. When a person truly loves, he has a natural desire to care (basic instincts). The desire to take care of each other is characteristic of happy families. ***Man expresses the care by responsibility for the woman*** he loves. Mutual affection for each other and feelings that have stood the test of time live and reinforce here. They say: "Marry is not a war. It's possible to return from there." But I sincerely wish you to meet the one and only, with whom you will be able to maintain affection and love for a long time. And no matter what I advise now, you will choose with your heart. And it is right. I hope it will be a man who will meet your expectations in the previous stages.

SMILE

A new book has been published - "Is it necessary to tell the wife about adultery? Advice from a traumatologist".

MINUTE OF WISDOM

I believe that any task, if approached with optimism and a positive attitude, can be accomplished.

Hillary Clinton

The pyramid has patterns

1. ***A man should feel loved*** - this is the only way he will have an incentive to move up the pyramid. But remember that everyone has his own love. And it is important to understand his expectations, his attitude to love. At the "Admirer" stage he should feel loved as a person who is pleasant to talk to. At the "Lover" stage, he should feel adored like a man. The top "Husband" is love-acceptance when we accept a person as he is. As it's said, "you have only yourself to blame!"

2. ***The initiative must belong to the man. Don't kill the initiative, and therefore the man in your partner.*** In nature, it is he who conquers new territories, and you master them (adjust to the circumstances)

and fill them with meaning. Leave him the right to feel leading in the relationship. Remember that the art of female intrigue, which men love in relationships (whatever they say), is half the skill of giving hints. The degree of their transparency directly depends on the intuitiveness of a particular object of your adoration. You can't make him marry you and you shouldn't. He is a man and he decides! But you can cause his irresistible desire to be with you all his life, the fear of losing you. It's in your power.

INFORMATION FOR REFLECTION

Three categories in the pyramid are three systems. Not the stages in a relationship, but the systems that can work at the same time and independently. After all, between a man and you there can be at the same time friendship, and passion, and affection, and sometimes only passion. You can start with passion and eventually fall in love, or you can just feel affection for a friend.

3. Don't pretend everything is going well if you feel like it isn't. Maintain adequacy in your requirements and do not rush things, but it is necessary to hint about your expectations, and if something goes wrong, tell him. Of course, in a form pleasing to him. After all, if you are always happy with everything, then there is no need to do anything for you! This is how a man usually thinks. It is better to talk in time so as not to reproach later. Most men don't have psychic powers (fortunately!). It is very important to correctly formulate your needs and verbalize them at every stage of the relationship. Ask about his expectations. Think about how they correspond to your desires and dreams. When people can just sit down opposite each other and freely talk about important things, this is the basic prerequisite for true love.

4. Place the "red flags". You need to learn to defend your principles with words, although men react better to the absence of words (then they start looking for an answer to the question: "Why did she shut up?") than to their abundance, and, most importantly, with the behavior.

If a man violates the boundaries of what is permissible, he goes to a lower category, and your attitude, consequently, changes. He will again need to complete his candidate program to move up. For example, if your husband violates your principles, be very polite with him, too busy with the diversity of life, become seductive and unpredictable, as in the "Lover" stage. Well, he'll have to strain again to get your attention. By the way, this same technique can help fight boredom in relationships. Your beloved has become sad and has already begun to look around - arrange for him the romance and unpredictability of the period of amorousness, play flirt with him.

SMILE

- You are sly, Ivanushka. If to marry - you are czarevitch, but when it comes to going to the army - you are just a goosey.

5. Learn to be friends with your admirers. Not all admirers will become husbands or lovers, not all lovers are capable of making friends, but this is not a reason to deny yourself the joys of life. Some men may be interesting only for romantic dates, some - only as pleasant companions. But a man who consistently goes through all the stages will be a good husband. The main thing is to give time to yourself and to him. And remember that the foundation is important in any home. And the base here is friendship. After all, passion passes, and in order to maintain devotion and affection for many years, a person needs to know that a reliable friend is nearby.

Coach exercise "Did I give a promise to love to the right one?"

You will have much more control over the situation when clear criteria emerge. Ask yourself questions, think carefully about the answers, feel them, use your intuition, remember the positive and negative experiences and write them down.

Four main questions for each of the three levels of the pyramid

ADMIRER
How do I imagine my admirer? Who is he?
(1-3 nouns, 3-5 adjectives.)

_____

_____

_____

What do I want to get from him? What needs do I want to satisfy?

_____

_____

_____

How can I understand from his actions that I get it from him?
2-3 phrases with verbs for each need.

_____

_____

_____

What does he get in return from me? (I remind you that only by giving,
we receive.)

_____

_____

_____

LOVER
How do I imagine the ideal lover? Who is he?
(1-3 nouns and 3-5 adjectives.)

_____

_____

_____

What do I want to get from him? What needs do I want to satisfy in a
relationship with him?

_____

_____

_____

How will I understand that I get this? (2-3 phrases with verbs for each need.)

_____

_____

_____

What do I give him in return?

_____

_____

_____

HUSBAND
What are my requirements for a candidate? What should he be?
(3-5 adjectives.)

_____

_____

_____

What do I want to receive from him? What needs to satisfy?

_____

_____

_____

What are his actions that speak of love and fidelity?

_____

_____

_____

What does he get in return?

_____

_____

_____

Strategic questions for each level
How can I let a man know about my needs?

_____

_____

_____

How will I provoke and stimulate his desired behavior?

_____

_____

_____

What will I never let a man do? (Taboos and "red flags" at every stage of the relationship.)

_____

_____

_____

SMILE

- Many people ask how I managed to quit smoking. It's incredible, but I just stopped putting cigarettes in my mouth and lighting them. It worked!

Three buttons of influence on men

Knowing the "three magic buttons" of male psychology, you can easily win the attention of any man, and later it will be easier to make him fall in love with you. By the way, these buttons are useful not only for women in a romantic search but also for those who are already in a relationship. These are the triggers that cause the release of testosterone in men and therefore make them feel masculine.

Button No 1. You're right!

The golden phrase to win the heart of a man. Each person is right in their own way. And when you agree with the opinion of another, you kind of pay him a tribute of respect, you emphasize his importance. By the way, the most important reason for parting, according to women, is often a lack of attention, and according to men - a lack of recognition in a relationship.

Button No 2. Sex

We adore romance and men adore sex. Of course, sexual harmony in a couple is important for both, but it is for men that sex is an absolute indicator of his "I can!", And the understanding that a woman "wants him" is a special topic for joy and pride in herself.

By the way, sex does not exclude romance, and romance does not exclude sex. Why deprive each other of joy?

Button No 3. You are needed!

Sometimes we are afraid to admit that "we can't live without him", because we are so independent, so modern and sarcastic. But in our hearts, we remain girls desperately in need of care and affection. We like men who care about our comfort and well-being, solve our everyday problems, and get rid of doubts. So let them do it and feel needed.

If you press these "three buttons" in a relationship with a man, he gets the most important thing from you - the FEELING OF HIS IMPORTANCE! And this is the most valuable thing in relationships for men if you want to feel like a real lady next to a true gentleman and a knight of your heart.

Women's charms, or the Magic of a compliment

Every man dreams of being charmed. And if I was asked about the universal advice for women who dream to charm, I would definitely answer: **admire the chosen one.** It is the **EGO that is the part of the man, with the stimulation of which he will be ready for feats!**

The ego is both the strongest and the weakest side of his personality. The feeling of self-worth, the desire for self-respect and self-realization drive men. And, if you want to manage the situation and win over your gentleman, *learn to do the exercise "Massage of the male ego with soft paws." By mastering the art of compliments, you will find the shortest and most effective way to his heart.*

As a rule, it is not customary to pay compliments to men, and therefore they are often perceived by men as flattery. This means that a compliment to a representative of the stronger sex should be special. Here are some tips on how to do it right.

Praise for his actions. "A man is not words, a man is actions!" Any, even the smallest heroic deed (for example, crane repair) is worthy of admiration. At the same time, it will serve as an incentive for new achievements.

Support his ambitiousness. If a man has achieved a lot, then he was very purposeful. If he has not achieved yet, it means that he will achieve next to a woman like you, who is able to inspire and note his successes.

Ask for advice. This is also a compliment. After all, you will not ask for advice from an inauthoritative person for you.

Note his friendship. A man is a team player by nature, and if he chose great friends, it means that he is not bad too.

Ask for help. He is so strong! .. It costs nothing for him to help a weak woman.

Adore him with your glance. Look at him from time to time, as if you are ready to eat him or with gratitude. Sometimes just an admiring glance is enough to cheer up a man.

Make him a defender. Feel confident next to him. For example, you are not afraid to walk in the park at night with him. Cuddle up and say that it's good and safe with him.

Be proud of him. Note that women pay attention to him. When you are walking, draw his attention to this. Let him know that you are proud of him.

Sing the praises. Do it with friends, relatives, acquaintances, when he is around and when he is not. Let's hope they will pass the information to him.

He drives amazingly. So all men think of themselves. You would never park like that! So tell him about it. (It's true, by the way.)

Compare him with an actor or character from the book for some masculine qualities, abilities, appearance. It's always nice to be compared to a celebrity.

Admire his voice. You are always pleased to hear it. And he will start calling more often to pamper you.

Note his great taste. In clothes, in choosing a car brand or drinks. In the end, he has chosen you! And this is irrefutable proof of impeccable taste.

Praise his character traits. Especially purely masculine, as well as optimism and a sense of humor. It's always nice to be in the company of positive people - let him consider himself so in your presence. *Appreciate his intelligence.* After all, it's so interesting for you to be with him, he knows so much! You like smart men, that's why you're with him.

And the most important compliment is the magic phrase "Yes, you're right!" Never argue so as not to evoke feelings of hostility. On the contrary, try to agree with him more often. In words ... And then do what is convenient and comfortable for you.

Compliments should not be rude or far-fetched. After all, we remember some of them all our lives, so try to be creative. Let your words become unforgettable, as well as you, their author. So you can become for him the best of the best, the only one who managed to understand and appreciate him!

SMILE

Patient: Hello, doctor. I have problems.

Doctor (writes something in the medical history): Sit down, little guy. Tell me.

Patient: I have ... a blank look. And my right shoulder twitches.

Doctor (continuing to write): Valerian and two pills of whateverin before bed - and as if by magic, as if by magic.

Patient: But that's not all. At night I dream that I am building underground pyramids in Tuscany. I am terribly concerned about the safety of the frescoes and the behavior of the binder solution in contact with groundwater.

Doctor (raises his eyes): What are you saying? How do you reinforce the foundation? I highly recommend twisted in four hardened rods, for centuries, you know, a run-in technique.

Patient: Doctor, something is wrong. On the identifier, the phones of people who did not call me, all the words on the signs and posters that the eye catches are cognate. My hamster does not talk to me for the fourth day, he sits motionless in the corner of the cage and looks at me with the eyes of a Balrog aiming at Gandalf with the tip of his whip.

Doctor (putting down his pen): What, however, a well-read animal! Have you tried to give him Russian classics?

Patient: And also, doctor, it seems to me that I feel and understand WOMEN!

Doctor (dropping glasses on the table, in an undertone): Oops!...

Collection of inspiring phrases for men

Words and phrases to support a man in his best qualities manifestation.

You're right!

Thank you for everything you do for me!

I am happy that I have you!

I know you can!

Please, advise me!

It is impossible to puzzle it out without you!

Well done!

You are on the right track!
Great!
You have figured it out!
Amazing!
This is exactly what is needed!
Sumptuously!
Congratulations!
Perfectly!
I'm proud of you!
Epic win!
I'm happy!
Unforgettably!
Wow!
Your help is very important to me!
This is what I have been waiting for!
It's a joy to be with you!
It touches me deeply!
I need you!
Well said - simple and clear!
Everything that worries you, troubles and makes you happy is important to me!
Witty!
Talented!
My hero!
Every day you get better!
You have done a lot today!
Excellent!
Even better than before!
Teach me to do the same!
Awesome!
I can't do without you here!
Cool!
I knew you could do it!
Sensationally!
I need you just such as you are!
Inimitable!
Incomparable!

Nobody can replace you!
Beauty!
I am proud that you have succeeded!
It's like a fairytale!
Very clear!
I couldn't have done better!
Fiction!
Very impressive!
Great start!
I feel good when I am with you!

Coach exercise "Massage of the male ego"

Create your top 10 compliment phrases for the stronger sex representatives, which you will definitely give on occasion. Remember: a man must feel his exclusivity and your originality.

_____

_____

_____

_____

SMILE
Compliments for men:
- I feel so smart with you!
- You are so serious, thoughtful ... Probably from the conclusion?
- You have beautiful lipstick on your shirt.
- And I haven't even known that red socks are produced.
- Is your whole body so hairy or just your nostrils?
- Have you wet your shirt under your arms on purpose?
- Hands are so rough ... You are probably a writer.
- Can you drink the second bottle?
- You look at me like I'm already naked.
- It's good next to you, reliable. Do you still have a lot of money left?

The NOT rules of a self-confident woman

And now the magical NOT-rules for women that will help you turn into a self-confident woman and increase your importance in His eyes. Why NOT-rules? Because there is always a place for creativity in life and you should always remember behavioral flexibility.

1. DO NOT be afraid

... to offend, to say, to dislike, to lose, etc.

Fear is a bad ally! It blocks the ability to soberly assess the situation. It is under his influence that people commit rash acts. Or they do nothing at all, which is sometimes even worse.

2. DO NOT try

The more you try, the more you strain. The more uncomfortable the situation is. Relationships should develop naturally and easily. Remember, it will not be easy to stand "on pointe shoes with a white bow" all your life.

You don't need to seem better than you are - you already know that you are the best!

Do not invest in relationships more than He: more time, energy, emotions. Better "less" than "more"! A person appreciates what he deserves.

In the classic Karpman drama triangle, "rescuers" usually try to do good to everyone and do irreparable benefits from the inner desire to feel their own superiority over those for whom they are trying. Behind pity for a partner, a super-desire to accept and understand everything is not love, but codependency and psychological complexes.

MINUTE OF WISDOM

To avoid disappointment in people, it's necessary to get rid of illusions. Learn to accept people as they are. Perfect people don't exist. You can find good people, but even they are sometimes selfish, irritable, and gloomy.

Abraham Maslow, American psychologist

SMILE

Once, engineer Kolya comes back from work, tired, there is slush, cold outside ... He decides to hitch a ride. Land Rover of the latest model stops, the window is rolled down, the gorgeous blonde at the wheel asks:

- Where are you going?

- ... I live in Butovo, but don't worry ...

- No, no, it's OK, let's pick up my friend, I'll carry you to the house for free.

They have gone, pick up the friend, a brunette, no less dazzling, comes down, sits down next to them.

Blonde:

- Well, let's go to the store nearby and run Kolya?

They stop by the supermarket, buy a bucket of caviar, Hennessy.

They drive up to the house. Brunette:

- Listen, I don't want to litter in the car, maybe we'll go up to you for a drink, eat?

They go up to Kolya and have threesome sex all night. In 3 months, the brunette and the blonde meet at a glamorous party, one says to another:

- Listen, I a, so tired of everything, of all these singers, actors, fucking figures, I am sick and tired ...

- Oh, yes, tell me about it, I want something ... Something ... Listen, maybe we'll call Kolya from Butovo?

- Kolya ?! Kolya from Butovo! Cool! Do you think he will remember us?

3. DO NOT suffer

Melodramas are good only in movies. In real life, it is better not to get hung up on relationships, let your mood depend only on you. "Pathetic" and "attractive" are antonyms. Happiness cannot be suffered or earned, but you need to be ready to take it as a gift with pleasure. Relationships are necessary for joy.

The world is beautiful and diverse! In order to understand that there are other fish in the sea, you need hobbies, friends, and admirers. Good relationships with others make a woman feel successful and more self-confident.

INFORMATION FOR REFLECTION

Critical thinking is a way of thinking in which a person puts in doubt incoming information, his own beliefs.

4. DO NOT forbear

Stop forbearing in the hope that he will understand everything or everything will work out by itself. If you constantly have to endure something in a relationship, and you are afraid of "ruining everything", most likely it is a love addiction, not love. Agree only to what really suits you!

5. DO NOT hope

I understand that it sounds strange. We are used to hoping for the best, and we often encourage ourselves in such a way. I suggest replacing hope with expectation. The expectation is always a reaction, which means that you have done something and are now expecting. And hope is about the fact that circumstances will turn out in your favor. Circumstances do not develop in life by themselves, they are created by a person through his behavior, life philosophy.

Living with illusions and empty hopes is a luxury for an intelligent girl. Have the courage to see the real facts and build positive predictions for the present and future based on the actions of a man, and not on your own emotional desires or guesses. You need not to hope, but to know that everything will be fine!

6. DO NOT be jealous

Jealousy is an ugly, unnecessary feeling for a self-confident girl, and biologically it is more common for men (the instinct of territorial protection).

And this emotion is secondary. It is based on envy and anger. What are you envious of? What are you mad at? Change either yourself or your partner!

Stop controlling, do not force accountability. Give the illusion of freedom! An attempt to control a man is regarded as an attempt to dominate. And being "weak" in his eyes is beneficial for you!

7. DO NOT hesitate to ask

Gifts, confessions, actions, etc. Do not deprive a man of the pleasure of being a conqueror and feeling needed.

INFORMATION FOR REFLECTION

Typology of love

D. Lee developed a detailed typology of love:

1) eros - passionate love-hobby, striving for complete physical possession;

2) ludus - hedonistic love-game, not distinguished by the depth of feelings and relatively easily admitting the possibility of betrayal;

3) storge - calm, warm, and reliable love-friendship;

4) pragma - arises from a combination of ludus and storge - rational, easily controllable; cupboard love;

5) mania - appears as a combination of eros and ludus, irrational love-obsession, for which uncertainty and dependence on the object of attraction are typical;

6) agape - selfless love-self-giving, synthesis of eros, and storge.

For women, storgic, pragmatic, and manic manifestations of love are more characteristic, and erotic and especially ludus love is more characteristic for young men.

8. DO NOT dispute

It is generally not profitable to dispute, there are no winners in the dispute, because subjectively every person is right. But the "loser" will forever remember the unpleasant aftertaste from the loss, and at the same time from communicating with you.

Try to find out and understand the position of the other, and not "rip your shirt open", proving your case. Give up fighting for your correctness. You already know that this is so! Simply and calmly explain your position. Once. You're not looking for approval - you're self-confident!

9. DO NOT teach

Educate! Do you feel the difference?

10. DO NOT take offense

You can be capricious (sometimes as a game). You should not take offense, because "the resentment will kill us all". And this is the best case!

Instead of "resentments" and the accumulation of all kinds of psychological garbage and complexes, learn to talk about your feelings in relation to his actions (no need to generalize and get personal) immediately. Specifically and to the point. After all, all unspoken resentments ultimately destroy the relationship.

Do not take offense, but draw conclusions and make decisions. Do what you need, guided by real desires. Women with dignity do like that.

SMILE
The generous and strong girl threw bread at the duck to death.

11. DO NOT take the initiative

Be active. But leave the initiative for the man, from the point of view of role models for him this process is more natural. I am often asked what is the difference between being active and taking initiative? Let me explain with an example: an invitation to a restaurant or a date is an initiative. But to suggest an idea, to provoke an act of a man (for example, to say that you want to go to an Italian restaurant) is an activity. Who needs more? You or him? Remember, women's initiative kills relationships.

12. DO NOT pretend

In a relationship, the one who overacts loses. Be yourself! Don't pretend, but play. Easy and beautiful!

13. DO NOT sort things out

DO NOT find out if he loves. What for? After all, you are already sure that he is crazy about you! Give up the competition. You're beyond it! You're the best! So behave yourself! When one clings, the other breaks free. This is the law!

14. DO NOT PROVE

If you constantly need to prove something to someone, then you don't need to prove anything! The need of constant excuses, arguments, and evidence can indicate that you are in a relationship with a manipulator, and your feelings are cleverly manipulated. You need to stop and think about why you waste your time and nothing changes. Maybe you are with a person who does not suit you, or you do not use the right communication tools? Do not waste so much mental strength, it is better to look at the essence of the problem.

MINUTE OF WISDOM
Perhaps this is true self-confidence: the ability to look at the world without expecting a nod of approval from it.
Nassim Taleb

15. DO NOT fuss!

Do not strive to get "everything at once" - make changes in your life gradually. Remember, "water wears away the stone not by force, but by the frequency of the drip."

To change in a couple of days is an impossible task, but you can feel a little different, a little better than yesterday, even from today.

Start believing today that you are a woman worthy of the best, because YOU ARE THE BEST, not one of the best! You are worthy of Love and Happiness! Always remember this!

SMILE

If you meet a bear in the forest, pretend to be a she-bear. At least it won't bite you ...

Women's mistakes in relationships

I would like to share a collection of women's "blunders" in relationships that I have collected throughout my career as a psychologist and coach. You have allowed some of them in the past too. Reconsider them and gradually start following more successful and effective strategies.

1. To think that you will be loved for your spiritual beauty (and preferably at first sight).

2. To put things off because he made a date at the last minute.

3. Constantly think about how to please him.

4. To pay him too many compliments.

5. To start caring for him like a mother, to make him understand that you can become a good wife for him.

6. Always apologize.

7. To compete with other women for his attention.

8. To pretend, to try to be a good actress in order to get into a role that he should like.

9. To be embarrassed and to deny your worth, while accepting compliments.

10. To argue with him, to convince of something and persuade.

11. To be afraid of losing him.

12. To constantly show initiative in relationships: to make him dates, to call, to text.

13. To hope that he will change.

14. To demonstrate sadness, resentment, anxiety, and with all your appearance to make it clear that this is connected with him.

15. To be pessimistic.

16. To demand attention, dates, confessions, promises.

17. To dissolve in a loved one.

18. Not to ask about his life plans, interests, values because of fear to seem too curious.

19. To live in anticipation of his call, SMS, dates.

20. More often to stay at home in the evenings in the hope that he will call and invite you out on a date.

21. To forget about your hobbies and friends.

22. To talk a lot about yourself, heavily embellishing the information and trying to please him with all your might.

23. To constantly analyze everything he said.

24. To complain, to whine.

25. To try to please.

26. To ask leave.

27. To wait until he is the first to finish a conversation on the phone or say goodbye at a meeting, even when you are busy or you are not interested.

28. To talk only about what you think he is interested in, but what you do not understand.

29. To demonstrate your insecurity.

30. To constantly dream about him and how you can be happy when you get married.

31. To reply to his SMS immediately, whatever you are busy at that moment.

32. To try to find out how he treats you, often asking: "Do you love me?"

33. To write long SMS with a bunch of emoticons.

34. To try not to notice your mental discomfort when he is around.

35. To forgive him for inattention.

36. To have sex with him to keep him.

37. To teach.

38. To compare him with others or with yourself, not in his favor.

39. To tell the whole truth and all the negativity about yourself, because you are honest.

40. To make him justify himself.

41. To justify yourself.

42. To show that he has no competitors so that he should not worry.

43. To take an interest in exs.

44. To be jealous.

45. To control his life.

46. Not to ask for anything, for any favors, so as not to strain him.

47. Not to ask for advice.

48. To reduce all communication with friends to talking about him.

49. To demonstrate that you will be lost without him.

50. To consider him to be better and much more successful than yourself.

51. To treat him the way you would like him to treat you, and not the way he treats you in reality.

52. To believe words, even when his actions are contrary to promises.

53. To make it clear that your mood and future are in his power.

54. To dramatically change your life plans because your relationship is "the most important thing in the world."

55. To lie to yourself that everything will be fine, even if you are constantly unhappy with him.

MINUTE OF WISDOM

I no longer have patience for certain things, not because I've become arrogant, but simply because I reached a point in my life where I do not want to waste more time with what displeases me or hurts me. I have no patience for cynicism, excessive criticism, and demands of any nature. I lost the will to please those who do not like me, to love those who do not love me, and to smile at those who do not want to smile at me.

I no longer spend a single minute on those who lie or want to manipulate. I decided not to coexist anymore with pretense, hypocrisy, dishonesty, and cheap praise. I do not tolerate selective erudition nor academic arrogance. I do not adjust either to popular gossiping. I hate conflict and comparisons. I believe in a world of opposites and that's why I avoid people with rigid and inflexible personalities. In friendship, I dislike the lack of loyalty and betrayal. I do not get along with those who do not know how to give a compliment or a word of encouragement. Exaggerations bore me and I have difficulty accepting those who do not like animals. And on top of everything I have no patience for anyone who does not deserve my patience.

Meryl Streep

Coach Exercise "Relationship Analysis"

Bring up your failed relationship and think about what mistakes you admitted.
- Why did you act like that?
- What feelings and thoughts did you have at that time?
- What did you want? And what did you get in that relationship?
- What is really important to you?
- How can you react to similar situations in a new way to get new results?

Coach exercise "corrections of mistakes"

Now take an A4 sheet and line it up in three columns. In the first column carefully write down the actions from this list in which you caught yourself. The second column is the analysis of actions. Just ask yourself two questions about each item: "Why do I do this?" and "Do I get the expected result?"

If you do not like the result, fill in the third column. Start it with the words "I have decided ..." And then write down a new way of behavior and thinking. Come up with new rules! Write the top ten right here. Let's see how well you learned your lessons.

MY NEW RULES

1.
2.
3.
4.
5.
6.

7.

8.

9.

10.

For each, even the smallest, victory (observance of a new rule) and overcoming of old beliefs, praise yourself, reward yourself with some pleasant things. In psychology, this is called positive reinforcement, which any new habit needs. The main thing here is patience and a desire to change the situation for the better.

Parting with your favorite "trap" is hard, but at least try to change something and become happier. I believe you will succeed. Reason to help you!

SMILE
In the shop:
- Excuse me, you have not returned my change …
- I excuse you!

LESSON 12

Be wiser!
Achieve success with two the most important words:
Love and Kindness!

It can be often heard that a woman should be crafty. I saw a lot of crafty ... and deeply miserable ones. I especially remember one client of mine. Anya could be called an honored veteran of women's training classes. Not because of her age, of course, (she was no more than 30), but because of the amount of gained "knowledge". She perfectly mastered the art of manipulation and seduction, she knew how to hurt with gaze and how to set her leg of an impeccable length and shape properly. She used to invitingly throw her splendid blond hair back and had exquisitely sexy makeup. And it did work: she had an army of admirers, a little fewer lovers - but had NO happiness! Nor had she a loving man by her side. After all, no matter how much you pretend, no matter how much you play, the area of feelings is still very sensitive and you cannot truly give a person something you don't have inside. Firm confidence, harmony, and unfeigned joy are attracting real men and feelings.

And it's impossible to achieve happiness, to find inner peace and confidence without a deep understanding of yourself, defining your true but not imposed goals. I remember we'd been working with Anya for about 3 months. It was difficult to penetrate the armor of established patterns and habits (even to wean away from weaning her outrageous get-up was not so easy). As the result, she found the main thing - the Real Herself! Just six months after our classes, Anya invited me for a cup of coffee. Beautiful and elegant, with her ardent eyes, she told me that she was marrying the guy of her dreams. And she avouched to have met such a worthy man for the first time in her life, neither devising plans to capture nor bothering at all, she was simply herself, the one who had shown up under a heap of bright but fake patterns. I wished her female wisdom goodbye. I will wish it to you too, my dear reader! It is female wisdom, consisting of intuition and intellect, that makes a woman special. It is for wisdom that men value and love us. It is not given by birth, it is not taught at school, but it is necessary if you want to be successful and happy in love. A wise woman makes decisions and acts following the principles of Kindness and Love. Believe me, if you are kind and open you do not lose anything. This is because everything in this world reaches for the light and focuses on development.

Get better! Advance, try, change yourself! Be brave, more active, and never give up. Remember: the race is got by running

SMILE
A real intellectual wouldn't ever say: "She is as foolish as she's always been", he would say: "Time has no hold on her!"

How to get more from a man without manipulations?

We can directly influence somebody only in three ways:
- the way we look;
- the way we speak;
- the way we act.

You shouldn't bet on one thing apart. You are supposed to look convincingly beautiful, communicate, and act with skill. Effective communication is one of the most important tools in relationships. No, it is not manipulation, it is the art of assisting your man to make a decision, which is advantageous for you both.

Use psychological communication techniques to get what you deserve from relationships.

1. Be curious - talk about Him. Most of all, people like to talk about themselves, and surely about money, love, and health. We are willing to talk about ourselves for hours without losing interest in the conversation.

2. Persuade those who want to be persuaded, those ones who are interested in contacts with you. Don't waste your time on ungreat and impartial people.

3. Be patient. Sometimes it takes time for a person to come to a certain conclusion of your interest.

4. Learn to speak in questions. The one who asks is the one who rules. Learn to hear the answers, not just listen to them.

5. Good things can get you famous! Pay compliments and simple favors, give cute gifts just "for no reason". A human has a sense of gratitude at the genetic level. He will definitely want to repay kindness. Get to know a kind of favor you may ask a man for, and remember: the more time, effort, and means are enclosed in relations, the more difficult to part then.

6. Imagine yourself as a bridge between Him and his Dream! Get to know what a man wishes for, acknowledge his necessities and benefits he gets from you. Conceive the things you need as an opportunity for him to achieve his desires in a favorable light for him.

7. Pay compliments. The exercise "Massage of the male ego with soft paws" is very effective. We all like compliments, and we have warm feelings for the one who pays them to us. We unconsciously start giving credence to such a person. Just be quicker-witted, sincere, and catch all the positive things in him and his actions!

8. Manage expectations. In order to be persuasive, you need to realize the expectations of others and try to exceed them a little. Promise less than you can give and leave room for a surprise.

9. Give an illusion of freedom. Let him be himself! Let him be imperfect. He mustn't fulfill all your hopes and dreams for 100% or within the time period you expect him to. People have the right to mistake, nobody's perfect - accept the fact. The main point is to focus on the major thing and do not expect more from others than you are ready to forgive yourself in relationships. Show generosity! Kindness is always evident.

10. Make them miss you. Price is a relative concept. If you want people to hanker for what you may offer (communication, attention, meets-up, etc.), then make it rare and precious.

11. Restrict an offer to the time frame. If it's time to make decisions and you want him to act, you should arouse a sense of urgency in him. Isn't he ready to take actions now? Then when?

12. Program him for a positive! Control the images in his mind. By means of words (more descriptive adjectives) create attractive illustrations of your future together or/and his benefits. The man finds an incentive. Less talk - more tell.

13. Be honest. Sometimes, the easiest way to convince a person is to tell him the truth about him. This is something that others don't usually do. Speak the truth - without judgment or hidden intent. Be unusual, which means unforgettable.

14. Speak the same language as him. Resemblance gets people together. You trust your close ones. You have a lot in common! Notice and/or envisage your similarities. Use his words and expressions in your speech. People mostly enjoy talking to others as to themselves.

15. Be flexible! Literally and figuratively. The situation is controlled by the most flexible one. Learn from children, they are not always proud, but they perpetually know what they want. They may beg, take offense, cry, bargain, charm. Children are willing to change their behavior until they get what they want.

16. Learn to express your idea clearly. Men love logic. Simplify your speech to the maximum. Start important conversations with facts and end with practical benefits for him.

17. The best impromptu is a prepared impromptu. May your knowledge about his interests be your "ace in the hole". Jokes elaborated beforehand and interesting stories are also welcome.

18. Get to like conflicts. They often become a cleaning factor in relationships. It is like rain, which relieves breathing afterwards. Do not put aside an unpleasant talk - do not hoard negativity. Try to clear the things up immediately. There are two primary differences between conflict and scandal.

1) every conflict has a noble purpose (for the good of both).

2) the absence of insults and claims (there are some words which are difficult to vanish out of your mind).

Before the scheduled conflict takes place, ask yourself: "What will be the best outcome? What do I finally expect to achieve? Why do I need this conversation? "

19. Keep calm in conflicts. You will come off as a person handling the situation. People are drawn to a strong one.

20. Have no doubt in a successful relationship - and act accordingly. The one who emits confidence will be always persuasive to others. Believe in yourself, his love, and his good intentions. If you really have faith in your acts and desires, you will always convince people to do what they need and thus receive in return what you want.

21. Share your positive energy and it will be back more than once. I may advise you on an excellent energy exercise: during the conversation, try to imagine yourself in a cocoon of golden light. Fill it in with those positive emotions you would expect from the other one. Focus this light, like a spotlight beam, to the opponent, or, on the contrary, take him inside this imaginary light. This will help you to keep your attention straight on him and awaken his positive feelings. Owing to mirror neurons, people easily and imperceptibly copy the moods and feelings of others. Usually, barriers of a psychiatric defense drop when you start applying effective communication techniques. The man opens up and trusts you. You start influencing his mind and actions. And I am pretty sure you will use it for good only, and your relations will make a new and better sense!

A man likes to talk to others the way he talks to himself. The barriers mostly fall when you operate with effective communication techniques. People open up and trust you. You start influencing their minds and actions. But there is nothing worse than playing with other people's emotions. You must understand this and avoid prohibited tactics.

Coach-exercise "I love men!"

Relationships'failures are mostly the result of negative summary beliefs about the opposite sex. It follows that if you want to be more attractive to others, start observing the good things in them. Notice and stimulate positive qualities of men from your society and thus activate your personal life.

Develop womanhood in yourself not bitchiness

It is considered fashionable to be a bitch. Women's magazines make flashy guidances, resembling the advice given by the cartoon teacher from "Devil No. 13": "Love yourself - don't care a groat the rest! And success awaits you ahead!" Beyond a doubt, these words bear some truth, but one should not take them literally. Human intelligence is given to clarify shades. And love intelligence - to be happy! Back in the day feminists fought for their equal rights with men, but the idea of "bitchology" itself is to rise above everyone and everything. Great it may seem, but rapid is the growth of disillusioned ladies who are in search but fail to find real men yet. As a result they frequently find themselves at my consultations. Frustrated and unhappy, they seek an answer: where the real men are. Where? Owing to them, the species is dying as unnecessary. It is impossible to fit together an independent, cynical, almighty woman, along with that image of one who should be taken care of, performed feats for, and protected.

Bitches live life on their own terms: I love myself, I am delighted with myself, and I don't care for anyone. That is, everything worked out well for her, she is independent from others. But for some reason, she is very lonely. She may suffer stealthily or during her visits to a psychotherapist. And that all because of her internal contradictions. The truth is that she, like any other ordinary woman, wants to let herself relax, so that someone may take care of her, indulge her. She hopes to see the gratitude light in the beloved eyes for the delicious dinner she cooked, wants to love sincerely but not at the flow of commodity-money relations. But there is a fear of losing the image of a "girl without fear and reproach."

According to a sociological survey, men **value beauty, kindness, and responsiveness** more among the rest of feminine traits. They make a woman desirable and attractive to men. An "anti-bitch" has such advantages. And here are some tips below on how to become one.

Love yourself but don't show it off.

Try to be attentive to other people's feelings so for them to feel comfortable with you. Sincerity and compassion are highly valued.

Appeal to your achievements and advantages wisely.

At first, try to notice the best things of the opponent, but your positive qualities should be either casually mentioned or pointed out as if in the context of some interesting story.

Break the habit of constantly talking about yourself

Your life is undoubtedly full of events, but let the other one tell you about himself. You will be considered a charming interlocutor afterwards.

Always be glad for a man's call, attention, and meeting.

Sometimes (and therefore rarely) break your plans so to see him - thus let him feel his importance. But at the same time may he know: your life is interesting and full, and you are with him not out of boredom, but because so good he is.

You have weaknesses, don't be afraid to confess

But do that secretly, and let them be lovely (confessions "I like to eat at large quantities at night" aren't included here), show your dignity and make a man support you and help - well, at least with his advice or something.

And yes, stop living by the slogans from social networks: "This is a battery that has its plus and minus ends. But I'm perfect! " ***Men don't like perfect ones, they like the real ones.***

INFORMATION FOR REFLECTION

Professor of psychology Jack Schafer spent many years working as a special agent for the FBI. He says about a golden rule, which can help you to win any person over, just snap your fingers and turn on his charm. And it sounds like this: "Make the interlocutor like himself."

SMILE

They say a woman needs two things for being happy: a good husband and all the rest.

MINUTE OF WISDOM
One of the best parables of King Solomon

When King Solomon came down from the mountain, after meeting the rising of the Sun, those gathered at the foot said:

- You are a source of inspiration for us. Your words transform hearts. And your wisdom enlightens the mind. We are eager to listen to you. Tell us: who are we?

He smiled and said:

- You are the light of the world. You are the stars. You are the temple of truth. The universe is in each of you. Immerse your mind in your heart, ask your heart, listen through your love. Blessed are those who know the language of God.

- What is a sense of life?

- Life is a path, a goal, and a reward. Life is a dance of Love. Your destiny is to blossom. BE is a great gift to the world. Your life is the history of the universe. And therefore, life is more beautiful than all theories. Treat life like a holiday, for life is valuable in itself. Life consists of the present. And the meaning of the present is to be in the present.

- Why do misfortunes follow us?

- As a man sows so let him reap. Misfortune is your choice. Poverty is a human creation. And bitterness is the fruit of ignorance. By accusing, you lose strength, and by lust, you dissipate happiness. Wake up, for a beggar is one who is not aware of himself. And those who have not found the Kingdom of God within are homeless. The one who is wasting time becomes poor. Don't turn life into vegetation. Don't let the crowd kill your soul. Let not wealth be your curse.

- How to overcome adversity?

- Don't judge yourself. For you are divine. Don't compare or separate. Thank for everything. Rejoice, for joy works wonders. Love yourself, for those who love themselves love all. Bless the dangers, for the courageous gains bliss. Pray with joy, and misery will bypass you. Pray, but don't bargain with God. And know, praise is the best prayer, and happiness is the best food for the soul.

- What is the path to happiness?

- Happy are those who LOVE, happy are those who give thanks. Happy are the pacified. Happy are those who have found paradise within themselves. Happy are those who give in joy, and happy are those who receive gifts with joy. Happy are the seekers. Happy are the awakened ones. Happy are those who hear the voice of God. Happy are those who fulfill their destiny. Happy are those who have cognized Unity. Happy are those who have tasted the taste of the contemplation of God. Happy are those who are in harmony. Happy are the beauties of the world that have received their sight. Happy are those who open themselves to the Sun. Happy are they flowing like rivers. Happy are those who are ready to accept happiness. Happy are the wise. Happy are those who have realized themselves. Happy

are those who love themselves. Happy are those who praise life. Happy are the creators. Happy are those who are free. Happy are forgiving.

- **What is the secret of abundance?**

- Your life is the greatest jewel in the treasury of God. And God is the jewel of the human heart. The wealth within you is inexhaustible, and the abundance around you is limitless. The world is rich enough for everyone to become rich. Therefore, the more you give, the more you receive. Happiness is at your doorstep. Open up to abundance. And turn everything into the gold of life. Blessed are those who have found treasures within themselves.

- **How to live in the light?**

- Drink from every moment of life, for unlived life gives rise to sorrow. And know what is inside and outside. The darkness of the world is from the darkness in the heart. Happiness is the rising of the sun. The contemplation of God is dissolution in the light. Enlightenment is the shining of a thousand suns. Blessed are those who yearn for light.

- **How to find harmony?**

- Live simply. Do not harm anyone. Don't be jealous. Let doubt purify, not bring impotence. Dedicate your life to beauty. Create for the sake of creativity, not for the sake of recognition. Treat others as revelations. Transform the past by forgetting it. Bring something new to the world. Fill your body with love. Become the energy of love, for love spiritualizes everything. Where love is, there is God.

- **How to achieve the perfection of life?**

- Happy one transforms many. The unhappy ones remain slaves, for happiness loves freedom. Truly, joy is where Freedom is. Comprehend the art of happiness. Open up to the world and the world will open up to you. By giving up the opposition, you become a master. And, looking at everyone with love, he added:

- But Silence will reveal much more to you ... Just be yourself!

Parting words

Thank you for reading my book!

I hope these 12 lessons will turn into 12 steps to your prosperity and happiness. I know, I believe that my book will help you with this! Although, there is one prerequisite for your success: you need to put knowledge into practice and do all the exercises that you find in this book. So you will achieve the desired changes in your fate.

And I promise that every little success you make will become my pride in you! Write about it to my email: info@oksanashmid.com and you will bring joy to me, and I will definitely congratulate you on this success!

With love and belief in you
Oksana Schmid

P. S. Remember, you are worthy of Love! Don't settle for less than happiness!

Books worth reading

- Richard Wiseman. 59 seconds. Think a little, change a lot.
- Hal Elrod. The miracle morning.
- Loretta Graziano Breuning. Habits of a happy brain.
- 20 lessons of wisdom of DAO
- V. A. Geodakyan. The evolutionary theory of sex.
- Alex Leslie. The hunt for the male.
- Allan Pease and Barbara Pease. Why men want sex and women need love.
- Allen Carr. Easy way to stop smoking.
- Andre Maurois. Letters to the stranger.
- Anna Barsova. How to live the own life, but not someone's else, or personality's typology.
- Antoine de Saint-Exupéry. The little Prince.
- Anton Semenov. Developmental trauma. Why can't you live the life you want and what to do about it.
- Anvar Bakirov. Games in which women win.
- Aziz Ansari and Eric Klinenberg. Modern romance.
- Barry and Janae Weinhold. Breaking free from the co-dependency trap.
- Ben-Shahar Tal. Happier.
- Ben-Shahar Tal. The Pursuit of perfect.
- Bert Hellinger. Insights: Lectures and stories.
- Bradley Trevor Greive. The meaning of life.
- Brian Tracy. Move out of your comfort zone.
- Bryant Theodore. Self-discipline in 10 days: how to go from thinking to doing.
- Burns D. Feeling good. The new mood therapy.
- Carl B.Rogers. Becoming partners: marriage and its alternatives.
- Carol Dweck. Flexible mind.

- Caroline Arnold. Small move, big change: using microresolutions to transform your life.
- Chadayeva I. V. Do not feel embarrassed! Effective ways to deal with complexes, fears and addictions.
- Chris Bailey. The top10 lessons I learned from a year of productivity.
- Dale Carnegie. How to stop worrying and start living.
- Daniel Goleman. Emotional intelligence.
- David Servan-Schreiber. The Instinct to heal: curing depression, anxiety, and stress without drugs and without talk therapy.
- Deepak Chopra. Ageless body, timeless mind.
- Doidge Norman. The brain that changes itself.
- Doris Brett. More Annie stories: therapeutic storytelling techniques.
- Ekaterina Mikhailova. I am at home alone, or Vasilisa's spindle.
- Elkhonon Goldberg. The executive brain: frontal lobes and the civilized mind.
- Eric Berne. Games people play.
- Erich Fromm. The art of loving. An enquiry into the nature of love.
- Esther and Jerry Hicks. The astonishing power of emotions.
- Fiore Neil. The now habit: a strategic program for overcoming procrastination and enjoying guilt-free play.
- Francine Shapiro. Eye movement desensitization and reprocessing: basic principles, protocols and procedures.
- Gary Chapman. The five love languages.
- Geoff Graham. How to become the parent you never had.
- Gippenreiter. Yu. Communicate with the child. How?
- Hal Elrod. The miracle morning: the not-so-obvious secret guaranteed to transform your life (before 8 am)
- Harvey Mackay. Swim with the sharks without being eaten alive.
- Harville Hendrix. Getting the love you want: a guide for couples.
- Harville Hendrix. Getting the love you want: workbook.
- Ilse Kutschera. What's out of order here? Illness and family constellations.
- James Hollis. Under Saturn's shadow: the wounding and healing of men.

- Janette Rainwater. Self-therapy: a guide to becoming your own therapist.
- Jean Shinoda Bolen. Goddesses in everywoman. Gods in everyman.
- John Gray. The Mars and Venus. Diet and exercise solution.
- Jordan Ellenberg. How not to be wrong: the power of mathematical thinking.
- Konrad Lorenz. On aggression.
- Konrad Lorenz. So-called evil: on the natural history of aggression.
- Lafayette Ronald Hubbard. Introspection rundown.
- Lao Tzu. Tao Te Ching.
- Leil Lowndes. How to make anyone fall in love with you. - 1, 2.
- Leslie Cameron-Bandler. They lived happily ever after: methods for achieving happy endings in coupling.
- Louise Hay. You can heal your life.
- Lucien Lévy-Bruhl. Supernatural and the nature of the primitive mind.
- Lyudmila Petranovskaya. What to do if
- Lyudmila Petranovskaya. Secret support. Attachment in the life of a child.
- M. Litvak's books.
- Maltz Maxwell. Psycho-Cybernetics.
- Marc Lewis. The biology of desire: why addiction is not a disease.
- Marco Iacoboni. Mirroring people: the new science of how we connect with others.
- Marilyn Atkinson's books on coaching.
- Marina Melia. Success - a matter of private.
- Nathan Schwartz-Salant. The black nightgown: the fusional complex and the unlived life.
- Neil Fiore. The now habit at work: perform optimally, maintain focus, and ignite motivation in yourself and others.
- Nita Tucker. How not to stay single.
- Osho. Love, freedom, aloneness: the koan of relationships.
- Peter Bregman. 18 Minutes. Find your focus, master distraction, and get the right things done.

- Richard Bach. Jonathan Livingston seagull.
- Richard J. Wiseman. Rip it up.
- Richard, Szirtes Helen.101 things to do before you're old and boring.
- Robert D. Frager, James Fadiman. Personality and personal growth.
- Robert Anthony. The ultimate secrets of total self-confidence.
- Robert B. Cialdini, Noah J.Goldstein, Steve J. Martin. Yes! 50 scientifically proven ways to be persuasive.
- Robin Skynner. Families and how to survive them.
- Roger Hock. Forty studies that changed psychology.
- Sergey Shabanov, Alena Aleshina. Emotional intellect. Russian practice.
- Sergio Bambaren. The Dolphin: story of a dreamer.
- Sharon Wegscheider-Cruse. Learning to love yourself
- Steve Harvey. Straight talk, no chaser.
- Susan Cain. Quiet: the power of introverts in a world that can't stop talking.
- Tatiana Zinkevich-Evstigneeva. The Secret of femininity, or how a woman unleashes her power and becomes the mistress of her life.
- Tina Seelig.What I wish I knew when I was 20: a crash course on making your place in the world.
- Tom Butler-Bowdon. 50 Self-help classics: 50 inspirational books to transform your life from timeless sages to contemporary gurus.
- Tony Hsieh. Delivering happiness. A path to profits, passion and purpose.
- Virginia Satir. Step by Step: a guide to creating change in families
- Yuval Noah Harari.Sapiens. A brief history of humankind.

Movies worth watching

Coach recommendation

Watch movies consciously. Keep in mind the main phrase of the movie, write down your main perceptions, conclusions, and decisions after watching, so you will become wiser.

1+1	New in town
13 going on 30	New year's eve
17 again	Nights in Rodanthe
2 days in Paris	Noel
27 dresses	Notting hill
50 first dates	October sky
8 first dates	Office romance
9 ½ weeks	Once upon a time in America
A couch in New York	One fine day
A Dangerous method	Only you
A Fish Called Wanda	Ordinary miracle
A girl called Rosemary	Original sin
A good woman	Other people's money
A good year	Out of Africa
A little bit of heaven	Overboard
A lot like love	P.S. I love you
A thousand words	Paris or Perish
A united kingdom	Paris-Manhattan
A walk to remember	Pass it on
A wish come true	Patch Adams
About love: adults only	Pay it forward
About time	Peaceful warrior
Absolutely anything	Platon
Alfie	Pollyanna
Alibi.com	Pope Joan
An education	Practical magic
An unmarried woman	Priceless
And now... ladies and gentlemen...	Pride and prejudice
Angel-A	Quantum love
Anger management	R.A.I.D. Special unit
Anna Pavlova	Rabbit hole

Another woman's life	Rabbit without ears
Arlette	Rain man
As good as it gets	Rang / the parallel
At Middleton	Remember me
Automatic brain	Remember more, or how
Autumn in New York	to improve one's work
Bad teacher	Return to Eden
Barefoot	Revolutionary road
Battle of the sexes: in the animal world	Rhapsody
(BBC)	Roman Holiday
Beastly	Running on the sunny side
Because I said so	Safe haven
Becoming Jane	Secrets of love
Bedazzled	Serial (bad) weddings
Bedtime stories	Seven pounds
Before sunrise	Sex & Mrs. X
Before sunset	Sex and the city
Before we go	Sex, love and therapy
Being Erica (series)	Share your smile
Being Julia	She's out of my league
Bel ami	She's the man
Belle du seigneur	She's the one
Better cheating and the like	Shirley Valentine
Beyond borders	Shopgirl
Big	Shortcut to happiness
Big eyes	Sideways
Big is beautiful	Six ways to Sunday
Billions	Sleepless in Seattle
Bimboland	Sleight
Bitter moon	Sliding doors
Black book	Slumdog millionaire
Blended	Sonny boy
Blind	Spring, Summer, Autumn, Winter...and
Blind date	Spring
Blue Jasmine	Spy
Body chemistry, hormone hell - (BBC)	Status single
Body. Chemistry. Love. (BBC)	Step up
Brave	Stepmom
Braveheart	Stoker

Breakfast at Tiffany's	Stranger than fiction
Bridge to Terabithia	Suckers
Callas and Onassis	Suits
Callas forever	Sweet November
Carmen	Talk to her
Casablanca	Tears in the rain
Casino Jack	Tender is the night
Cast away	Thank you for smoking
Catch me if you can	Thank You for the Chocolate
Catherine	The accidental husband
Catwoman	The adjustment bureau
Certain women	The age of Adaline
Changeling	The age of innocence
Changing sides	The age of reason
Chaotic Ana	The aviator
Chasing happiness	The back-up plan
Cheri	The barber of Siberia
Christmas Cottage	The beauty of Amelie
Cinderella	The best of me
Click	The best offer
Coach Carter	The blind side
Coco before Chanel	The bridges of Madison County
Confessions of a shopaholic	The bucket list
Confessions of a sociopathic social	The butterfly circus
climber	The butterfly effect
Cool runnings	The change-up
Crazy stupid love	The chef
Cruel intentions - 1,2	The cherry on the cake
Dalida	The confirmation
Dangerous beauty	The curious case of Benjamin Button
Dangerous liaisons	The devil wears Prada
Dates	The devil's advocate
Dating the enemy	The duchess
Days of summer	The edge of seventeen
Dear John	The English patient
Desert flower	The experiment
Diary of a nymphomaniac	The face of love
Dirty grandpa	The family man
Dirty rotten scoundrels	The fault in our stars

Divorce a la Francaise	The first wives club
Dorfman	The game
Dorian Gray	The geisha
Down with love	The girl on the bridge
Dukhless	The girls
Duplex	The global brain
Eat pray love	The golden age
Educating Rita	The greatest love
Elegy|	The green beautiful
Elizabeth	The hangover
Elizabethtown	The holiday
Enchanted	The hot chick
Enough said	The Human Mind
Erin Brockovich	The imitation game
Far North	The invention of lying
Feast of love	The intern
Florence Foster Jenkins	The iron lady
Fly me to the moon	The Italian
Focus	The Joneses
Formula of love	The kid
Forrest Gump	The king's speech
Frances Ha	The lake house
Frankie and Johnny	The legend of 1900
French kiss	The longest ride
Frida	The love witch
Furtseva.The legend about Freaky	The lover
Friday	The lucky man
Friends with benefits	The man from U.N.C.L.E.
G.I. Jane	The marrying man
Gambit	The matrix
Gandhi	The mirror has two faces
Ghost	The most charming and attractive
Grace of Monaco	The nanny diaries
Grey gardens	The notebook
Groundhog day	The other Boleyn girl
Going the distance	The other side of midnight
Good will hunting	The other woman
Gone with the wind	The Painted Veil
Groupies don't stay for breakfast	The piano

Hachi: a dog's tale	The prince of tides
He's just not that into you	The princess and the warrior
Head in the clouds	The Pokrovsky gates
Heartbreakers	The proposal
Hector and the Search for Happiness	The queen
Her	The rebound
Hitch	The secret
Holy man	The secret: dare to dream
Homecoming	The Shawshank redemption
Hope Springs	The skeleton key
How do you know?	The Social Network
How to be single	The Soul Keeper
How to get smarter, think faster	The Spanish apartment
How to lose a guy in 10 days	The story of us
Hunting and Gathering	The stranger
Husbands and wives	The strangers
I could never be your woman	The sweeter side of life
I feel pretty	The sweetest thing
I'm staying!	The taming of the scoundrel
If I loved you	The terminal
If I were a boy	The Thomas Crown affair
If tomorrow comes	The time traveler's wife
Imposters	The Truman show
In her shoes	The truth about exercise (BBC)
In the mood for love	The ugly truth
In your eyes	The valet
Indecent proposal	The valley of light
Indignation	The very merry widows
Inside I'm dancing	The very same Munchhausen
Inside out	The vow
Interstate 60	The walk
Intimacy	The wedding planner
Intolerable cruelty	The wedding singer
It begins with the end	The white queen
It's a boy girl thing	The words
It's Complicated	The young Victoria
It's kind of a funny story	There's something about Mary
Jackie	Things to come
Jane Eyre	This means war

Jerry Maguire	Three steps above heaven
Jesus loves me	Titanic
Jet lag	To Rome with Love
Jewtopia	Tootsie
Jonathan Livingston seagull	Tristan + Isolde
Just Friends	Tycoon
Just go with it	Two for the road
Just like heaven	Two moon junction
Kate and Leopold	Under the Tuscan sun
Knight and Day	Unfaithful
Knockin' on heaven's door	Up in the air
Kramer vs. Kramer	Valemont
Kung Fu panda	Velvet
La dame de Monsoreau	View from the top
La la land	Vicky Cristina Barcelona
Last chance Harvey	W.E.
Last holiday	Wag the dog
Last Night	Waiting for the miracle to come
Leap year	Wall street
Legend #17	Water
Letters to Juliet	Water for elephants
Lie to me	We're the Millers
Life is beautiful	Wedding unplanned
Like water for chocolate	What about Bob?
Lost in translation	What dreams may come
Louise L Hay. You can heal your life	What happens in Vegas
Love	What the bleep do we know!?
Love Actually	When Harry met Sally
Love, Rosie	While we're young
Loving	Who's afraid of Virginia Woolf
Lucifer	Wild orchid
Mad money	Wings of desire
Magic in the moonlight	Yes man
Maleficent	You've got mail
Mamma Mia!	Young adult
Man up	Zoe
Marley & me	
Master of the game	
Match point	

Me before you Me two Meet Joe Black Men of honor Message in a bottle Michael Midnight in Paris Mona Lisa smile Moonlight tariff Morning glory Mr. & Mrs. Smith Mr. destiny Mr. nobody Mr. Stein goes online Muse My best friend My best friend's wedding My brilliant divorce My life in pink My mom's new boyfriend My name is Khan My one and only	

RECOMMENDED MUSIC

For reducing the feelings of anxiety, uncertainty in a successful outcome
Chopin. Mazurka and Preludes
Strauss. Waltzes
Rubinstein "Melody"
For general calming and tranquility
Beethoven Symphony No.6 part 2
Brahms "Lullaby"
Schubert "Ave Maria"
Schubert. Andante from quartet
Chopin "Nocturne in G Minor"
Debussy "Moonlight"
For reducing irritability, disappointment
Bach. Cantata No. 2
Beethoven "Moonlight Sonata"
Prokofiev. Sonata in D major
Franck. Symphony in D minor
For relieving the emotional intensity with people around you
Bach. Violin Concerto in D minor
Bartok. Piano Sonata
Bruckner. Mass in E minor
Bach. Cantata No. 21
Bartok. Quartet No. 5
For mood improvement
Chopin. Prelude
Liszt "Hungarian Rhapsody No. 2"
For increasing serotonin level (depression treatment)
Paul Collier "Serotonin Activator"
Schubert "Ave Maria"

Handel. Aria from the cantata "Dettingen Te Deum"
Faure "Lullaby"
Dvorak "Slavonic Dance No. 2"
Tchaikovsky "October - Autumn Song"
For relieving the nervous intensity
Bizet "Pastoral", "Old song"
Leclair. Sonata in C major, part 3
Faure "Elegy"
Saint-Saens " The swan"
Gluck. Melody from the opera "Orfeo and Euridice"
Lei "Love Story"
Lennon "Yesterday"
Glazunov "Intermission" from the ballet "Raymonda"
Tchaikovsky "Barcarolle"
Shostakovich. Romance from the movie "The Gadfly Suite"
For general comfort
Beethoven. Symphony No. 6, part 2
Brahms "Lullaby"
Schubert "Ave Maria"
Chopin. Nocturne, Lullaby, Barcarolle
Chopin. "Impromptu Fantasy"
Liszt "Consolation", nocturne
Tchaikovsky. Nocturne
Mozart "A little night serenade", Symphony No. 40
For reducing anxious feelings
Strauss. Waltzes
Chopin. Mazurka, preludes
Rubinstein. Melodies
For getting out of a disappointment, irritability, awakening of feelings of belonging to the beautiful world of nature
Beethoven "Moonlight Sonata", Symphony in A minor
Bach. Cantata No. 2
Tchaikovsky "Sentimental Waltz"
For the treatment of hypertension
Bartok. Piano Sonata, quartet No. 5
Bruckner. The mass in A-minor
Bach. Violin Concerto in D minor, cantata 21

For relieving from overextension headaches
Liszt "Hungarian Rhapsody No. 1"
Mozart "Don Juan"
Khachaturian. "Masquerade Suite"
Beethoven "Fidelio"

For the treatment of insomnia
Mozart-Fleece "Sleep, my joy, sleep"
Dunaevsky-Lebedev-Kumach "Sleep comes to the threshold"
Ostrovsky-Petrova "A cricket sings behind the stove"

For quick information digesting and enhancing the mental working capacity
Mozart, all works

For attention focusing, better concentration
Schumann "Dreams"
Debussy "Moonlight"

For creativity stimulation
Khachaturian "Dance with sabers"
Dunaevsky. March from the movie "Circus"
Ravel "Bolero"

For raising general vitality, improving mood, state of health, activity
Beethoven. Overture to Egmont
Liszt Hungarian Rhapsody No. 2
Monti "Czardash"
Sarasate "Navarra"
Tchaikovsky. Waltz from "Serenade for String Orchestra"
Tchaikovsky. Symphony No.6, Part 3
Chopin. Prelude No. 1, opus 28

For struggling with despondency, sadness, depression, recovering peace of mind
Beethoven "Ode to Joy" from Symphony No. 9; sonata "Appassionata"; "Moonlight sonata"

For getting out of a sense of fear
Vivaldi. Suite " The four seasons"

www.ingramcontent.com/pod-product-compliance
Lightning Source LLC
Chambersburg PA
CBHW021619120626
46545CB00001B/311